Can We Be
FRIENDS?

REBECCA
FRECH

Heidi —
So glad to have
you in my 150
bless you!

Su
Vi
www.osv.com
Our Sunday Visitor Publishing Division
Our Sunday Visitor, Inc.
Huntington, Indiana 46750

D1473092

Our Sunday Visitor Publishing Division
Our Sunday Visitor, Inc.
200 Noll Plaza
Huntington, IN 46750
1-800-348-2440

ISBN: 978-1-68192-262-1 (Inventory No. T1950)
eISBN: 978-1-68192-263-8
LCCN: 2018932966

Cover and interior design: Lindsey Riesen
Cover art: Shutterstock

PRINTED IN THE UNITED STATES OF AMERICA

About the Author

REBECCA FRECH is a Catholic author, speaker, CrossFit coach, and the managing editor of The Catholic Conspiracy website. She is the author of the best-selling *Teaching in Your Tiara: A Homeschooling Book for the Rest of Us*, a co-host of the popular podcast *The Visitation Project*, and a columnist for the *National Catholic Register*. She and her husband live just outside Dallas with their eight children and an ever-multiplying family of dust bunnies.

Dedication

For Kara, who still loves me even though I write books.

Contents

Introduction

"Life is nothing without friendship."
— Cicero

W hen I first began thinking and talking about writing this book, I was surprised at the reaction of the people I had mention it to. It didn't seem to matter who they were, when I said the word "loneliness," their own tales of being and feeling isolated would pour out. Almost everyone, it would seem, is lonely.

I've spent a lot of time thinking about the loneliness that seems to run rampant in our world. Never in history have people been more connected than we are now. We're all walking around with easy access to almost every person we've ever met. A scroll through the directories on our phones nearly always turns up someone to talk or chat with. Silence and time to ourselves are now completely optional. Our phones come with us everywhere (if you have kids or a dog, you don't even pee alone anymore!). Which has many of us wondering: If I'm never by myself, why do I feel so lonely?

We're not meant to be solitary creatures. Way back in the beginning, God looked at Adam and declared that it wasn't good for man to be alone. It wasn't long before God created Eve. They had a couple of kids, and then a few more. Those first people could have spread out and gone anywhere, but history shows us that they mostly stayed together. They congregated in tribes and then towns, not just for safety but also for companionship. Fast-forward thousands of years and we're still congregating, not just in person, but in virtual villages and communities. Still, we're left wondering, How can a society that centers on constantly being connected have so many people feeling as if they are all alone?

I started my research where I usually do, with a call to my grandmother. Ninety-six years old and still sharp as a tack, she's a treasure-trove of common sense and wisdom. "I'll tell you why y'all are all so lonely these days," she drawled. "It's on account of three things — air conditioning, television, and women drivers."

I waited for her to explain what she meant, and with a sigh she said: "Back before air conditioning, it used to be just too darn hot to sit inside on a summer afternoon and evening, so we didn't. We sat outside on our front porches with a big pitcher of sweet tea and visited with our neighbors. We knew the names of everyone living up and down our street, and there was always someone there if you needed them. It's not that way anymore. It's cool and comfortable in your homes, so you go inside and sit in the cold air. You're bored or lonely because the people in your television talk to you and keep you company, so you never actually have to spend time with any real people at all."

She thought for a moment and then said: "But what really did you in was women drivers. Once women started driving and folks got a second car, people started driving their kids all over the place. Used to be that kids played in the neighborhood or did sports at the school. Now y'all are driving them an hour each way for ballet or soccer or goodness knows what else, and patting yourselves on the back for being good mothers. It seems to me that you've traded having a life of your own for your kids' being busy. That doesn't seem like a very good trade to me."

She was right, of course. She's always right. It goes so much further than air conditioning, television, or women drivers (none of which are bad things, of course, and, actually, they're all pretty good). Almost everything in modern life seems designed to keep us alone and lonely. How did it get this way?

After talking to Grandma, I started Googling. I kept running across the terms "Dunbar Number" and "Dunbar Theory" as explanations for what's going on in our modern relationships. British anthropologist Robin Dunbar has spent years studying human social interactions and has come to the conclusion that we all have a finite number of people we can fit into our social circles. For most people, that magic number is around 150. That's everyone from your spouse and children, to your relatives, to that guy from high school that you keep up with on Facebook. It doesn't matter how long your list of "Friends" is, you can't maintain relationships with more than a total of 150-ish.

A hundred fifty people is a lot of people to keep up with, but it used to be much simpler. Most people lived in the same place for the whole of their lives. If they did happen to set off for somewhere new, they left their social network completely behind and constructed a new one for themselves wherever they happened to be. They became completely enmeshed in the fabric of their new community. The people they knew mostly knew one another, and friendships overlapped and wove around one another, creating a densely woven society. We don't do that any longer.

These days, we are a much more mobile society, but we don't really leave anyone behind. Instead, we maintain our social and emotional ties to people through social media and technology. Relationships that would have died natural deaths in the past now don't ever have to end. We grow up and leave for college, taking with us all of the people we knew and loved throughout our childhoods. We gather a few more in college and elsewhere along the way. We keep adding people to our circle, but the number of relationships we can actually maintain never changes. Eventually, we end up somewhere and settle down with room for just a few spots left in our circle.

Even worse, our people don't know one another. They may not even know of the others. Our relationships no longer interweave; they're more like the random pattern of a shotgun blast. The kind of community that people were designed to live in no longer exists for most of us. There are all kinds of gaps between our relationships — and those are the cracks that we end up falling through.

That's when we begin to notice how quiet our social lives have become, and how much we really want and need to have friends and people near us. We spend more time on the phone or on social media trying to connect or reconnect with the people we miss, and we bemoan the fact that we can't find people "here." All the while, we avoid getting to know our neighbors, calling back that guy from work, or joining any clubs or church groups. The thought of meeting all those new people is a lot to deal with, and we start saying things like, "I don't have the time or energy for meeting people right now." And we're right. Our social abilities are strung out and filled by the people we have clung to for no reason other than that we knew them back in the day. Hanging on to those people we've known forever is a big part of the reason we all feel so alienated and alone today. Let them go, and set yourself free.

Then, once you've purged your friend list and cleared your social calendar, the search for your tribe can begin. But where? It has to start with knowing ourselves and who we are when all the layers are stripped away; not the person we pretend to be when we're with other people, but the authentic self. A friend of mine once told me, "A good friend will let you into their life; a great friend will let you into your own." Isn't it time you found people like that?

CHAPTER 1

A Case for Friendship – Why Do We Even Need Friends?

*"Friendship ... is born at the moment when
one man says to another 'What! You too? I thought
that no one but myself ... '"*
— C. S. Lewis

I curled up with my nine-year-old son on the couch as he cried out the hurt he had suffered from his best friend's decision to "unfriend" him. He sniffled and sobbed and wiped his runny nose on my sleeve. "Why do we even need friends?" he asked me. "What are they even for?" I struggled to explain the purpose of friendship to someone whose heart was so freshly broken and came up with a "mom speech" that was not quite right. The fact is, it was a good question, and one for which there was no easy answer.

After a lot of reading and research, and asking even more questions, I've learned that once upon a time friends and community were necessary for survival — there was no way for a guy to kill a mammoth with a stick unless he brought his buddies with him. We've evolved past hunting our food with sharp sticks, thank goodness, so what roles do our modern friendships fill? And, are they somehow necessary for our survival?

I asked my eldest daughter — conveniently, she's a neuroscience student — for the scientific purpose of friendship, if there was one. She began by explaining that human beings are herd animals and therefore have an instinct to congregate in groups for safety. She explained the evolution of the brain with a lot of very big words that I wrote down to look up later. Now that I have, I'm still not sure I understand. What I did get out of that conversation, though, was that there seems to be a biological drive to create friendships. So, there must be a purpose behind them.

The need for people and community is hard-wired into our psyches. Studies of human brain activity show over and over that the presence of a close friend releases dopamine, serotonin, and oxytocin into our brains. Those are the "pleasure" hormones, the same ones that make us fall in love and keep us from killing our children (always a benefit!). We don't merely get silly or goofy when our friends are around; we get high. Suddenly, my high school and college shenanigans make a lot more sense.

What I keep coming back to is the idea that we still need our friends and family for safety and survival, just maybe not the physical kind. Because of the internet and technology, it's absolutely possible to work from home, shop from home, bank from home, and have everything we need to keep our bodies functioning delivered right to our front door. There are now services that will even bring your purchases inside your house, making it unnecessary to even step outside onto your front porch. We practically never have to interact in person with another human being ever again. As a result, many of us have become quasi-hermits. We huddle inside the home theaters in our McMansions, eat the dinner that was delivered, build ten-foot-high fences so we don't even have to acknowledge that our neighbors exist, and text with our virtual friends all night long. (Heaven forbid we should actually call someone.) Then we wonder why we're depressed and living under the oppressive weight of this modern loneliness.

It's because we need people. We're herd animals, remember? We may not be out hunting big game with our Cro-Magnon posse, but that doesn't change the fundamental fact that we are designed to live in community and have relationships with other people. We need our friends to help keep us emotionally, mentally, and spiritually healthy. Just as nutritious food feeds and energizes the body, our friends feed and energize our minds and souls.

My grandmother is known to remark, "If I want to know who you are, I'll just look at the company you keep." I didn't really understand what she meant until middle and high school, when I saw how the good kids I knew were influenced into doing some pretty bad things. Their reputations were ruined because of the people they hung out with on the weekends. There were crowds of nice kids, and gangs of "the other kind." In our smallish Texas town, your character was judged by the crowd you ran with, and it was extremely hard to salvage your good name once it was tarnished by hanging with troublemakers. There's a reason for it, of course. The fact is, most of us will allow our character to rise or fall to the level of the people around us. Therefore, we should surround ourselves with good people.

Over the years, I have learned to discern which friends are worth investing my effort, time, and energy in, and which aren't. I stopped looking at surface qualities, such as looks, age, or social standing, and began to look instead for people who made me laugh, brought me joy, gave me the gift of their honest selves, and weren't afraid to tell me the truth when I screwed up. I love meeting new people, seeing who they have in their own inner circles and how they treat them. (My grandmother was right: You can tell everything by the company your friends keep. So, pay attention.)

Friends are there to bring out our better selves

Close friends can also serve as our own Jiminy Cricket, pricking our conscience and fueling our better natures. They may be quick with a joke that raises eyebrows and makes us snort with laughter, but they also make us want to stretch and become the best people we are capable of being. When I was a small girl, my mother told me that the mark of a truly great friend was that they would make you want to be a better person; if they didn't, then they weren't really that great a friend.

My best friend and I keep each other on the straight and narrow by calling each other out on our crap. She doesn't let me get away with anything, and I return the favor. We listen to each other's excuses when we aren't as good as we ought to be, and then we say: "That's a great excuse. What's the real reason?" We're hard on each other, but God help the person who criticizes us, even if it's ourselves.

On a particularly down day a few years back, I cut into her "I'm not good enough/patient enough/whatever enough" diatribe to tell her: "No one gets to be this mean to my friend, not even you. You may be frustrated right now, but you're talking about the friend I love, and I'm not going to listen to her being run down like this."

She laughed and sighed, but this has now become a standard thing in our friendship — we don't let people talk trash about others, not even about ourselves. Instead, we say, "Yeah, I get it — this is hard right now — but here's where you are killing it ..." Those reminders of all the places we're actually succeeding, even when it seems as if the sky is falling, have pulled us out of plenty of tailspins.

Because we're so close, we get to see the patterns in each other's lives, the patterns we don't often see for ourselves. That gives us the perspective to tell each other hard truths, like, "Every time you spend time with your sister-in-law you become a lunatic crazy person" or, "Spending time with your mother makes you eat all the things; maybe you should clean out the junk food and stock up on carrots before she comes over" or, the painful to hear, "You suck with money; maybe you need to take a class on money management or turn the checkbook over to your husband." Who else is going to tell you this if it's not your friends? Who else is going to be close enough to the daily living of your life? Who else wants you there hanging out with them in heaven so that they're willing to make "being amazing" a group project?

Henry Ford was known to say, "My best friend is the one who brings out the best in me."

Exactly so.

Good friends help keep us calm and out of jail

There are days when the whole world seems to be working right on my last nerve and I become the teapot from the nursery rhyme: "When I get all steamed up hear me shout ..." Boom. Then my head explodes, and I word vomit all over the person next to me, savaging them with the venom of my anger. Or I call my best friend and rant about the state of the world, how much I detest bureaucracy, and how "I'm just done with it all! Done, and I mean it!" She'll quietly sip her coffee and listen before she goes to work helping me figure out the whole stinking mess.

For the past fourteen years, Kara and I have been the confidante and sounding board for each other. We are the voice of reason, peeling each other off the ceiling, talking the other off the edge of the cliff, and cooling boiling tempers. The ability to help balance us out and remind us of our better natures is part of why having what Anne-with-an-E Shirley called a "bosom friend" is so valuable (my first Green Gables reference in this book). Throughout our lives, there will only be a small handful of people we will trust with the whole truth of who we are, and who will trust us in return. These people are valuable and necessary to our own good mental health. They are the friends we trust to be honest with us — and to protect us from the worst we can be.

They help us chase our dreams

There is a woman I know who took seventeen years to get her college degree. She took her first class when she was nineteen and finally walked across the stage at thirty-six. Along the way she got married, had three children, and moved as a military wife a half-dozen times. But she stuck with her studies. Her friends were there for every step. They listened to her plans and dreams, helped her study for tests, and supported her through the days when she wanted to walk away from it all. On the day she finally graduated, they filled an entire row in the stands and screamed her name as she was handed her diploma. Her victory was also theirs.

Good friends don't let you quit on your dreams for yourself. They know that being static isn't growing, and not growing isn't being alive. There is nothing more exciting than watching the people you love fight and claw and work their way toward the impossible dream, and then watching them actually achieve it. Friends don't let you sit quietly in the corner and fade into a beige version of the person they love. They push, cheer, and cajole you into seeking and dreaming, and help drag your exhausted carcass over the finish line.

They help keep us healthy and alive

Studies consistently show the health benefits of having friends. People with close friends are less likely, on average, to develop diabetes, heart disease, depression, and dementia. People with close, meaningful friendships live longer, on average, perhaps because they're having too much fun to die.

Studies on pain tolerance have shown that having a friend nearby after surgery actually lowers your perception of the pain you're in and means you need fewer drugs to cope. That means friends are a painkiller, which is kind of like a superhero, so that's pretty cool.

It's been proven that the emotional ties of close long-term friends and the mental stimulation they provide are even more effective than exercise in protecting long-term health! Having friends is better for your health than having a gym membership and giving up ice cream. That doesn't mean that you don't need to exercise, of course, just that it would be even better if you dragged friends along, or made friends while you were working out. And no one should really give up ice cream.

Good friends encourage us on our walk with God

I want to go to heaven, but I don't really want to be hanging out on those cloud benches and listening to the angelic choirs all by myself. While that would be great, it would be even better if my friends were there with me, singing along. We pray for and with one an other and with each other all the time. We discuss theology and parse our way through what we each believe. We know that part of being healthy is being spiritually healthy, and we want that for one another more than anything.

Any time I find myself in the middle of a period of chaos and upheaval in my life, my friend Jen can be counted on to say: "When was the last time you went to confession? Your life always goes sideways when you haven't been going." What's remarkable about that is that she's not Catholic. She doesn't stop to think about what she believes. She knows the things that are part of my walk with Christ, and she can see the peace that the sacraments bring me. While we don't see eye to eye on theology, we've both got our gazes firmly fixed on Jesus.

Good friends aren't shy about holding each other accountable if one goes off the road and starts drifting into sinful behavior. Faithful friends rejoice over God's blessings for the other and are bold in crying out to him on each other's behalf. During the most difficult times of life, a good friend will be like Simon of Cyrene, helping us to carry our cross. They truly want what's best for us and know that that ultimately means heaven. They help us work toward our own salvation even as we help them toward theirs. Friends are brothers and sisters in Christ, and that makes us family.

We are witnesses of one another

My ninety-six-year-old grandmother puts it even more simply: "Our friends serve as the witnesses of our lives. They are there to remind us of the things we have forgotten and the tales we've lived along the way. When we are gone, they tell the world that someone like us once lived and loved. Then someday, hopefully, they will come to stand before the Throne of the Almighty and argue on our behalf. On that day, may their tongues be true and their memories a little faulty." Amen.

CHAPTER 2

What Is a Friend?

"In poverty and other misfortunes of life, true friends are a sure refuge. They keep the young out of mischief; they comfort and aid the old in their weakness, and they incite those in the prime of life to noble deeds."
— Aristotle

We've gotten lazy with the word "friend" in the past few years. A word that used to mean a person you were close to, or "the family you choose for yourself," has become slang for anyone (and everyone) we know. "Can you recommend a plumber?" I have a friend… "Do you know anyone who goes to that gym?" I have a friend…

Of course, these people aren't really friends. They may be nice enough, but they're only people we are familiar with through life or social media — people whose names and faces we happen to know.

Our grandparents used to call such people acquaintances, and I'm all for breathing new life into that word. There's nothing wrong with being an acquaintance and not a friend. It simply means that you're not invested in each other's lives. I don't know my plumber's favorite movie, where he hopes to retire, or anything about his family. I do know that he snakes a mean drain, that he's fast and efficient when the pipes go wonky, and that he charges me reasonable prices. I don't really need to know my plumber any better than that. He seems to be a nice guy, but he's not my friend.

I'm also not friends with my next-door neighbor, the guy who mows the grass, most of the people on my social media "friend lists," or even my best friend from junior high school. Thanks to modern technology, I may be able to tell you what they ate for dinner last night and where they went on their last vacation, but that knowledge merely creates an illusion of companionship. None of us actually knows each other as people. "Liking" someone's Facebook posts and posting birthday greetings when social media prompts us to do so is not the same as a real relationship, and somewhere inside of us we all know that.

So, what is a friend? Simply put, it's someone to spend time with, enjoy, depend on — someone with whom you share your life. It looks so simple on paper, but a deep friendship can actually be a very complex relationship. Part of that stems from the fact that there's a wide range of people between those we just happen to know of, an acquaintance, and the kind of friend Aristotle called "one soul in two bodies."

Work friends

After acquaintances, most people we know tend to fall into the "work friend" category. Our work friends are the people we hang out with because we have one or more activities which regularly place us in close proximity. We're at the same place at the same time, so we chat and hang out because they are convenient to talk to or to do stuff with. They are people we probably wouldn't choose to hang out with on our own, but when in Rome … : the girl in your history class you grab a coffee with while you compare notes and study for the next exam, the coworker who may be a little older or younger than you but is also the only other normal person in your department, the only other mom at gymnastics class with no makeup and a messy ponytail who's not talking about when her three-year-old is going to be an Olympic gold medalist —

these are your people of the moment and your sanity in the midst of craziness.

While they're great for inside jokes and snarky commentary for now, they're probably not going to last beyond graduation, your next job change, or your princess deciding she's really more into karate than gymnastics. There will be many of these temporary friends during your life. You'll pick them up and then set them down again once your paths diverge, and there won't be any hard feelings about it. The glue that held you together will be gone. Five years from now, you'll see them online or at the grocery store and wrack your brain to remember: "I know I know that guy, but what was his name?" Don't worry about it, because that person will be doing exactly the same thing when he sees you.

Your kids' friends' parents or your spouse's/ significant other's friends

The parents of your children's friends and your husband or wife's friends are work friends who deserve their own category. You're going to be spending a significant amount of time with them whether you like it or not. You may not even have anything in common with them except that your kids are inseparable or you both like hanging out with your husband. Well, suck it up, because your opinion doesn't really matter here.

You're not in charge of these relationships, and it is likely you're in for the long haul. You're going to be emotionally invested in their families and welfare because it will directly affect your kids or your spouse. Hopefully, they're going to be cool, and y'all can just hang out, swapping embarrassing stories and stupid internet memes. If you're lucky, they'll move beyond the work-friend territory and become your friends in their own right. If not, that's okay, too.

Your inner circle

Work friends are great, but when we're assembling our inner circle, we look for a little bit more. We look for people to fill specific roles in our life, just as they are looking for people to fill roles in theirs. It may not even be an on-purpose decision, but it happens all the same. If someone posed the question, "Who is he to you?" your brain would think, "Now that you mention it ..."

When you are looking around for a new BFF, some of it is up to chemistry, but don't think that it isn't an intentional decision. Making friends is one skill, and choosing them is quite another. Picking the right people to be close to you is very important. The people we surround ourselves with rub off on us. We pick up quirks and habits, sayings and attitudes from them. We tell our children to be mindful of the crowd they run around with, and we need to do exactly the same thing.

When we're looking for friends, we all want people who are honest, understand our sense of humor, and stand by us. We don't usually think about the roles they are going to end up playing in our lives, but we should. We all have a few key slots to fill in our posse; here are a few of the most common:

The Sage
Oh, wise one, tell me what you know.

We all need people in our lives who are smart, inspiring, honest, and give great advice. These aren't the friends you take on wild adventures, but they can be counted on for a trip to the coffee shop and hours of deep conversation. We all need at least one friend who is a little older, more experienced, better read, or just flat-out willing to tell us the ugly, unvarnished truth. That's why we all need a sage.

Stuff is going to happen, and you'll need to be able to rely on the wisdom of someone else, because your own brain just isn't working or you have no clue what's going on. We need a friend that we can ask. Sometimes, we need to hear harsh truths from someone whose opinion we trust. That's why we need the smart, honest friend. The sage is the friend who will tell you that you can't make a living at underwater basket weaving no matter how good you are at it, and that maybe you should be pursuing a more practical career and not a hobby. She will also be the person who tells you that accounting is sucking the life out of you; that a girl who reads neuroscience books for fun might want to do something with that instead. When everyone you know just adores the boyfriend you've broken up and gotten back together with a dozen times, this is the friend who will tell you to knock off the games and get rid of both the drama and the loser guy, because you're too smart and pretty to be wasting your time this way. This is the friend who will have the courage to tell you that your life is a mess and maybe you need therapy more than new video games or clothes. He or she will like you enough to be brutally, and constructively, honest. He simply wants what is best for you and has no time for anyone standing in the way of that — even if the person in the way is you.

If you don't have a sage, go find one. If you are the sage for your friends, Godspeed, my friend. Keep reading, learning, and paying attention. The rest of us would fall apart without your wisdom.

The Bold Adventurer

As great as it sounds to spend the weekend in your jammies curled up on the couch binge-watching the entire series of *Gilmore Girls*, that's not really a life. Think how sad that would sound as an epitaph! That's why we need our adventurous friends. Our favorite adrenaline junkies drag us out of our comfort zone every chance they get. They drink deeply from the experiences of life and want to try almost everything at least once before they die.

While some of us feel the need to map out a plan and cover all the contingencies before we act, this friend just boldly leaps. She encourages us to stop focusing on being safe or indulging in our perfectionist tendencies to only do things when we can do them "right." Her life motto is "Throw caution to the wind, grab a wild hair, and just go!"

Your bold-adventurer friend sees exactly how big the world is and aches to explore it all. Yes, she can tire you out, but it's totally worth it. She's the reason you finally ate sushi, joined a gym, climbed a mountain, and floated down the Frio River.

Exhausting, but worth it, this friend will lead you through hairbrained adventures whose tales you'll be regaling your grandchildren with in years to come, or will merely get you off the couch into the bright sunshine. You're not a mole, and sunlight is a very good thing.

The Holy One

"Did you go to Mass this weekend?" "Can I pray for you?" "Can I pray with you?" God bless our holy friends. Compared with the adventurous friend, this one can seem a little tame by comparison, but don't be fooled. There is a depth and beauty to this friendship you won't find anywhere else. My holy friends are the ones I turn to when life gets wickedly hard and I need a reminder that I'm not alone. There is great comfort in knowing that whatever crud I'm mired in at the moment is just for the moment. As my favorite holy friend often reminds me: "I read the Book, and it all turns out right in the end. If it's not right, then this isn't the end." That kind of wisdom, the hours of deep soul-searching conversation, and the insistent nudge in the right direction make this friend a necessary one to have.

Your holy friend lives each day as if it's his last because he knows tomorrow isn't promised to anyone. He's constantly striving for heaven and would like nothing more than to have you walk the straight and narrow with him. If we become a reflection on the people around us, who couldn't stand to be a bit holier?

The Best Friend/Soul Mate

If my husband is part of my heart, my best friend is a big chunk of my soul. There are days when she's the only reason I'm sane. On days when the children are wild, dinner is burned, and the bank account is empty, she's the magic that keeps me going. Fourteen years of friendship and counting, she knows that I am one big old hot mess and still loves me anyway. She's the person I call while I'm waiting on the pregnancy test results, and I provide a voice of calm when she's waiting on hers. She's my confidante and conscience, my favorite cheerleader, and the team I always root for.

We only have room for one or two of these friends in our life at any given time, and to lose a best friend can feel like an amputation, as though you've lost a necessary part of yourself. These are the few rare friends who manage to cross over into becoming family, the ones we really, deeply love, and they become a part of our soul.

There's more to a group of friends than just having stuff in common, hanging out together, and having a good time. Have you ever thought about what it is that your friends love and appreciate about you? We all have our own place within our groups of friends, our own special niche to fill. Have you ever thought about who you are to the people you hang out with, and whether your people are acquaintances or something more?

Are you the mentor or the sage? Do your friends come to you for advice or for you to help them with life skills? Are you the comforter or the clown? Are you the caretaker or the adventurous one? If you're trying to talk everyone into climbing Mount Kilimanjaro next summer, or joining you in a CrossFit class, it may be blindingly obvious. If you're on your knees praying for the people you love and reminding them to get to confession, you probably have an idea who you are within your social groups. You may be filling one specific role, or a mishmash of three or four. The important thing isn't the label concerning where you fit in your relationships, but that you are in a role you're comfortable filling.

The people who make up our lives — the acquaintances, friends, work friends, and soul mates — are the connections that make up the fabric of our lives. We invest in others' lives and get happily tangled up in all of the big and small things that accompany that investment. These people add their own spicy flavor to our lives and help us to discover the person we never knew we always wanted to be.

CHAPTER 3

How Many Friends Do You Really Need?

"Kindred spirits are not so scarce as I used to think.
It's splendid to find out there are so many of them
in the world."
— Anne Shirley, *Anne of Green Gables*

"You really need only one good friend in life," my grandmother has repeatedly told me. "To expect anything more than that is just selfish." She's not wrong, of course; one really good friend in life is actually an amazingly huge gift. She and her best friend, Lou, literally knew each other their whole lives, and the tales of their shenanigans are legendary in our neck of the woods. They have entire conversations made up of single words, partial phrases, and meaningful looks that leave them doubled over in stitches or "hmmm-ing" in mutual disapproval. A friendship that's more than ninety years in length means most of the words are simply unnecessary. I agree with her. Expecting God to grant us more than one Lou in life would be selfish; it would also be a recipe for ending up in jail. Old ladies or not, there are shenanigans.

While I recognize the truth in what she said, it has never failed to make me feel sad and a little lonely to hear. The extrovert in me always asks: "Only one? That's all we get?"

Now that I'm a grown-up and have seen a little more of life, I can clearly see both her wisdom and where she was wrong.

Grandma's "one good friend" is a bare minimum. When God said, "It is not good that the man should be alone" (Gn 2:18) at the beginning of time, he gave Adam the starter set of just one companion. Eve may have been all Adam needed, but as soon as there were more people around, it's likely he didn't mind the extra company. It's also important to note the word "expect." Just because we shouldn't go around expecting God to gift us with more than the bare minimum, it's not wrong to ask for it. Ask God for all of the people you want, but recognize each one for the gift that he or she is.

Not everyone can be a Lou, and thank goodness for that. We really can't be super close with more than just a tiny handful of people at any given time, and usually not more than one or two. The anthropologists who study these kinds of things say that human beings can't have more than five best friends, ten regular friends, thirty-five acquaintances, and a hundred or so people you just happen to know. Even that seems like a lot for anyone who's a decade or more beyond college.

If you read the Introduction (and if you didn't, you really should) you'll recall that people are only capable of caring for approximately 150 people at any given time. That includes best friends and acquaintances, as well as all of the people you sort of keep up with through your mom or social media (like your ex-best friend's nerdy younger brother and that girl you sat beside in the third grade who ate the paste). If you can tell me what they named their dog, where they went on vacation last year, or what their kid was in the school play, you know too much information to pretend that you don't care; they're in your circle. If you're keeping up with your favorite reality TV stars with this same level of involvement, your brain may not realize that you don't actually know them and may be placing them in your circle, too. That's some valuable give-a-crap real estate to be turned over to people you were just "following."

A hundred or so "give-a-craps" may initially seem like a lot, but it fills in pretty quickly. There's more than just that third-grade girl who ate paste in that big group (she became a doctor, by the way). The people who fall under the acquaintance umbrella also include our prayer circles and support groups. This isn't a group of people we barely know or that most of us would be willing to do without.

Even though there can be a pretty high turnover in our circle of acquaintances and give-a-craps, we like having them around because they can turn out to be pretty important. Let the stuff start hitting the fan and suddenly those people on the periphery of our lives morph into our safety net. When our middle daughter became a paraplegic a few years ago as a result of a medication side effect, that give-a-crap group joined our closer friends and family in rallying to our side. They contributed enough money in twenty-four hours to buy her wheelchair and were tireless in helping us chase down specialists and answers. They arranged Masses for her and sent us e-mails and letters of love and support from around the world. Over three years later, we're still hearing from the people who once were "people we used to know" or "internet people we'd never met in real life." These people may not be our main support system, but they were definitely our people. Just because the group is large or not in your inner circle doesn't mean that they're not a big deal. They definitely can be.

Which brings us to our friends — not our best friends, but a step closer to us than our acquaintances. You're probably not going to have more than a dozen people in the friend zone. Your friends are mostly a fluid group, with individuals moving in and out, depending on what's going on in either of your lives today. People in the friend zone tend to "step forward or back," depending on who is suddenly fun to be around or who has dropped out of favor for being annoying as heck. Our friends tend to fall into loose categories, such as "the people I work out with" or "people I can call at the last minute for an adventure." They're your group, but not your inner circle. They're in your life for a good time, but not necessarily for a long time.

At last we come to the chosen few — the ones who have seen you ugly cry and whom you have seen at their worst, and yet y'all still love each other anyway. The experts may say you can't have more than five BFFs, but that seems like a lot to me. Most people I know have between one and three very close friends. (This is the one that Grandma was talking about!) Your best friend is your sanity walking around, the only person you will always answer the phone for, unless you're in church. My best friend has been with me (on the phone) as I took the pregnancy tests for my youngest five children. You know someone loves you when they're okay with listening in while you pee on a stick. (That's a delicate balancing act, by the way — phone in one hand and pee stick in the other.) She's the only person I'd trust in a moment of such vulnerability, and, of course, I've returned the favor. Someone this close is as essential to our lives as breathing. From cradle to grave, we need that person (or two) to walk with through life.

Our circle of friends actually looks a lot like the concentric circles of a target, with us at the center. The closer people are, the smaller the circle gets. Can you imagine if you had to spend the same amount of time and energy on the give-a-craps as you do your lifelong best friends? That would be exhausting. Who has the emotional stamina for such a thing? There's a reason why Facebook has to remind you of most people's birthdays, and why you don't wish all of them a happy one. The relationship you have doesn't justify the outlay of energy and effort it would take to know when those birthdays are off the top of your head. That kind of commitment is for the people you see regularly — and your mother, because God help you if you forget your mama's birthday. Only the Almighty can save you from that.

CHAPTER 4

Stop Waiting to Be Asked

"Friendships unfold gradually as women share intimacies with one another — this takes time. You need to be willing to let your friends know the real you. But you don't want to spill your guts out the first time you're out to lunch."
— Irene S. Levine

When we were kids, making friends was easy. March right on up and introduce yourself, and if they didn't insult you or ignore you — boom, friendship. My five-year-old daughter found her best friend at the neighborhood pool this summer with a conversation that went:

Hi.
Hi.
Your hair is beautiful.
I like your swimsuit.
Want to play with me?
Yes. Want to be my friend?
Okay.

Although, to be fair about it, if someone started off a conversation with me by saying how pretty I was, and they weren't creepy, I'd be their insta-friend too. I'm a sucker for an opening line like that.

In junior high, girls rose and fell in popularity based upon their social circles and hence became more mercenary in their relationships. A brave few would cleave to their elementary school friends even when popular opinion declared them uncool. But it takes a strong preteen to be willing to swim against the tides of public opinion. The middle school years are a brutal lesson in politics and pecking order — one very few of us would willingly repeat.

Making friends acquired more nuance in high school. Friendship was less about proximity and more about what we had in common. Things like faith, ethics, and whether or not we had the same kind of crazy strict parents came into play. As teenagers, our time with our friends was spent less in active play and more in hanging out. Words and conversation and the exchange of ideas became the foundations of our friendships. Even though the relationships might have changed, the pool we drew from was still the same. We found our people at school, church youth groups, or in the neighborhood, and our friends still looked remarkably like one another. Same age. Same stage of life. Same conversations. Our friendships were exciting, and exactly what we needed at that point in our lives, but for most of us there wasn't a lot of variety going on.

As adults, friends are much more difficult to find. We don't step out of college into a world filled with other new adults ready to take on the world. Instead, most of us step into jobs, careers, or stay-at-home parenthood, and the people we find aren't necessarily anywhere near where we are in life. For the first time in our lives, it's both socially acceptable and likely for us to have friends who are completely different from us.

Up until adulthood, we had only to look around and pick out the people we wanted to be our friends. But all of a sudden, the options seem to disappear. Instead of looking around, we have to actively seek out potential friends. It's no longer a smooth transition, but work. For maybe the first time in our lives we have to go looking. We have to start making an effort.

We have to start "dating." Then comes the realization that if we want to build a community, this is what it's going to take. Since most of us lose half of our friends every seven years and replace them with new ones, we're going to be dating for friends for the rest of our lives.

Adult friendships are scary. Let's just admit that so we can move on. They're really scary. To be friends as adults, you have to lay it all on the line and be open about what kind of weird you really are, and, honestly, we're all some kind of weird. This means that if someone turns down our friendship, there's a decent chance that it's personal. It could be that there is something they don't like or decide it isn't worth their effort. Getting shot down by someone is awful. No matter how you slice it, it stinks.

It's not just a fear of rejection that makes us hang back, though. By the time we're grown, most of us have had some experience with users, abusers, and toxic friendships, and we don't want to be burned again. Way back in the day, I explained to my eldest daughter that dating was "going out with a bunch of different people to decide what's acceptable to you in a life partner." I think the same holds true when you're dating for friends.

You can't find what you want until you know what you're looking for

Most of us have never consciously considered what it is we're looking for in our friends. We may know it instinctively, but may have never put it into words before. While most people have a list of attributes we want in a spouse, we don't have a corresponding list for a BFF. It wouldn't hurt to make one.

Get out a pen and paper and start asking the hard questions: What kinds of people are you naturally drawn to? What kinds of people do you enjoy hanging out with? Are there any habits or attributes that are absolutely nonnegotiable? Or absolutely intolerable? What kinds of things do you like doing with your friends? Do your friends need to be at the same experience level you are at, or are you willing to teach/learn? Don't stop and think about it; just write the first thing that comes to mind.

As you're answering those questions, is there someone who pops into your head? If you're not already friends with that person, is there a reason why?

If no one sticks out right away, that's okay. That just means that you're starting fresh. You're making a kind of wish list, like a form on a dating site or a letter to Santa Claus. As with letters to Saint Nick, though, you're probably not going to get everything you ask for. If you're lucky, you can get pretty darn close, or you may find that the friend you need isn't what you think you want at all. That's okay. This is just a place to start.

Once you know whom you're looking for, it's helpful to have an idea where you can find people like the ones on your list: places or groups that you can or do go to — church, clubs, classes, social-media groups, etc. If you're not already a regular, you might consider becoming one. This isn't elementary school — you're going to have to actively go out and meet people.

Finding friends isn't something you have to do all by yourself, though. As with dating, ask your family and current friends if they know someone. Be willing to go on a "blind date" or two, and accept all invitations. If someone you already love thinks enough of someone else to set you up or pass along a phone number, you might as well give it a shot. Going out for coffee or meeting up for a movie isn't a lifetime commitment.

You're going to have to flirt a little

When we meet people we think like, but don't know yet, we all flirt a little. It lets us learn about the other without jumping into a commitment. We play with words, joke and tease, and banter back and forth. Just like when dating, friendship flirting gives you the opportunity to figure out whether or not you have chemistry with someone else, and if your values match up. Flirting with a potential new friend slows the train down long enough to feel out the relationship. If it doesn't work out, you have protected your heart and there's been nothing between you but play. If it does, then you know that it has the potential to be a friendship that's really worth investing in. Flirting may just be the most important step in creating new friendships, so slow down and savor it.

Things are getting serious

If you have found someone you think might be more than just an acquaintance, and potentially long-term, you've gotta court them. Don't worry, courting is not just for the Duggars, and you don't have to ask Jim Bob's permission for anything. When you take away the odd reality-TV connotations, courtship in dating means that you're learning more about each other and moving purposefully toward something more permanent.

Courting is a time to delve deeply. That means it's appropriate to ask "all the questions." It also means you're going to have to answer all the questions. It can be quite tempting, as my mom says, to always put your best foot forward, only to tell the good things about yourself and hope that a potential friend doesn't see the messy bits. It's tempting, but don't do it. We all have embarrassing stories and character flaws, and thank goodness for that. Perfection is boring. It's the imperfections that make us uniquely ourselves, so don't be afraid to be yourself.

This is the time for vulnerability. When people feel fragile and uncertain, they start to lean on others. That lean is a good thing. If you can trust each other with the crap from your pasts, it is a good sign that you'll be able to lean on each other when it all hits the fan again.* Don't think it won't, because this is life, and life is messy.

If there are any warning signs or red flags that this relationship might be unhealthy or have the potential for taking a toxic turn, you're probably going to find it here first. Tell your own truths, but make sure that you pay attention to what is said. My mom is fond of saying: "God gave you two ears

---

* If there's something you truly don't want your friends to know, that's probably something you need to discuss with a licensed therapist. Don't let stuff like that fester. Take care of it and get on with your life.

and one mouth. You should listen twice as much as you talk."
I've never found the situation in which that's not good advice
to follow.

It's time to play

When we're adults, life tends to tilt toward the serious side. It
seems as if there's always another chore that needs doing or
e-mail begging to be answered. Getting bogged down by your
to-do list is easier than falling off a log. While any friend worth
having is going to be willing to jump into the trenches and
help you fold the never-ending pile of laundry covering your
sofa, if that's all the entertainment you ever offer, good luck
finding someone to stick around for that. You've got to do a
little wooing.

Coffee dates. Workout buddies. Thrift-store adventures.
Get out of your own space when you can and see the world
together, even if the world is limited by how far you can go
until the babies melt down. What kinds of things do you like to
do? What harebrained schemes have you been dying to try? It's
time to dust off your bucket list and drag it out into the light of
day. Doing stuff together creates shared memories and inside
jokes. An epic road trip that included freezing temperatures,
a broken heater, beignets in New Orleans, and the Tastee 29
Diner means that my friend Scottie and I have only to say
"New Year's in D.C." to send the other into peals of laughter
and inappropriate eyebrow wagging. We all need someone we
can inappropriately waggle our eyebrows at, but you can't have
one unless you have the memories to back it up. Go play.

What you want to find out

At the end of the day, what you're looking for is relatively
simple. You want to know if your potential new bestie is
someone you could take a twelve-hour road trip with and not
want to strangle her before you get there. You need to know if
this is a person you can rely on in a crisis, and the even harder-
to-find someone who will still be around when your life is
ordinary and boring. The only way to know whether or not a

friendship is worth pursuing is to try the relationship on for size. Is it uncomfortably constricting, or does it give you room to be yourself?

While life is always intrinsically valuable, it can be a long, hard, and lonely road. The right people can make the journey joyful. When we were children, finding the "right people" was as simple as discovering someone willing to share their Cheetos. If you're lucky, the Cheetos-sharer is still walking beside you. If not, that's okay. There are people out there in the world looking for someone like you to do life with. You've just got to go find them, and that means you've got to date.

CHAPTER 5

You Say "Alone" As If That's a Bad Thing

"People think being alone makes you lonely, but I don't think that's true. Being surrounded by the wrong people is the loneliest thing in the world."
— Kim Culbertson, *The Liberation of Max McTrue*

I don't think I had ever been as alone in my life as I was the summer we relocated from Oklahoma to Dallas. We'd left friends and loved ones behind to move back to the Lone Star State, and while we did know people in Texas, they were still eight or more hours away. My children quickly ferreted out the other kids in the neighborhood (as children do) and were off exploring the creek at the end of our street or playing upstairs in our game room with new friends almost every day. I was busy unpacking boxes and arranging our lives, so I stayed at home in the silence. When you're used to the cacophony of living with six children and a husband, the aloneness of "all by yourself" can be a shock.

I wanted to get out and start exploring our new city, so I waited for the weekends when my husband would be home to go with me. I could have taken the children and gone, but that seemed more like a chore than leisurely wandering. So, I would eagerly wait for Saturdays and the chance to have someone to wander with. I was so used to having someone by my side to talk to and explore with that the very thought of going by myself sounded lonely and sad.

Then an art exhibit came to town that I was dying to see, but my family didn't share my enthusiasm. Instead, they looked horrified that I would want them to come with me. "Why don't you just go by yourself?" my husband asked as he shooed me out the door. So I did. As I slowly meandered my way through the art gallery, I realized that I'd been wrong. Going it alone wasn't necessarily something I had to avoid at all costs. There was definitely an upside to going solo.

You get to be the master of the clock

If I had brought anyone else to the art exhibit, I wouldn't have felt free to glide past certain pictures and really drink in others. I would have had to be considerate of what my companion wanted to see and do. Instead, I was able to spend almost an hour sitting on a bench in front of the most astounding portrait, gazing into the subject's eyes and studying every crease and fold of the skin on his hands. I didn't need to see anything else. I needed time to reflect. That one painting had been enough of an experience for me to make the trek downtown worth it.

Being by myself made me the master of the clock and the keeper of the schedule. I didn't have to ask if anyone else was finished and ready to go, if they were hungry, or if I was rushing them. I started when I wanted to, and finished when I was done. No explanations and no apologies. That's not something you can do when you're with someone else and still be an acceptable person — unless you're a two-year-old.

You pick the restaurant

I've come to the point in my life at which "What do you feel like eating?" is the most boring question in the world. Nobody can ever agree, and if the consensus isn't what you want, then you have to make do. That isn't always easy. It's hard to be happy at a seafood place when what you are really craving is a great burger. (You can usually find a decent burger in most places, but a great burger is almost spiritual. It's difficult to find the holy kind of hamburger at a place that specializes in fish.) You end up finding something on the menu that sounds okay enough because the outing is usually more about the people you're with than it is about the food.

But if you're by yourself, then it's all about the food. Without the obligation for conversation and politeness, eating out can be a gustatory revelation. You can savor every last crumb and scrape the sauce from the plate (if that's your thing). Just make sure that the waiter puts you at a table out of the way so no one else has to witness your love affair with your dinner. Get the extra garlic. Dawdle over the crème brûlée. Lick the spoon in an unseemly fashion. Your mother isn't at the table, and neither is anyone else. There's no one to offend, so suck down that chocolate like Augustus Gloop. Then sit back with a Cheshire Cat grin. If you find yourself thinking, "It's too bad _____ isn't here; he would love this place," don't worry, because that means you get to come back and taste it all over again.

Ironically, eating by yourself often means that you eat less. Time and again, studies have shown that people eat more when they are with other people. There's some dispute over whether the reason is social pressure to eat as long as the other people at the table are, or if you keep eating because your attention is on the conversation and not whether or not you feel satisfied. I don't know that the cause really matters. The effect of solo dining is that you consume fewer mindless calories. If you're going to indulge yourself, it's better to have it be on purpose and not because your best friend's husband just won't stop talking.

You can just stay home

The word "alone" conjures up an image of someone sitting at home on a Saturday night. There's only something wrong with that if you want to be somewhere else. If home is a comfortable and safe place to be, why wouldn't you want to be there? After a long day of work or errands, or hours spent surrounded by other people, there's nothing shameful about enjoying time alone.

Alone means that you can binge-watch Netflix and pause the shows in the middle of the action if you have to pee. It means eating ice cream straight out of the carton and swigging the orange juice straight from the bottle right out in the open because there are no witnesses. Alone means you control the remote, or the Wand of Power, as we call it at our house, so you can rewind and watch your favorite movie scenes fifteen times if you want to. Alone makes home a "you do you" environment. No apologies, because there's no one to apologize to.

Everyone needs time alone

Let's discard the idea that being by yourself makes you some kind of failure. It doesn't matter who you are or what your life looks like, everyone needs alone time. If it's your regular state in life, that doesn't mean you need to go collect someone just to fill in the gap. That's not fair to you or the temporary people you would gather. The best friendships are intentional, not merely "good enough for now."

Being by yourself means you have the opportunity to explore your interior and exterior life without the encroachment of another person's opinion. It means that you have the gift of silence to explore your own thoughts and get to know who you are on your own, rather than becoming defined by your relationship to another person. Who are you, after all, when you're not being someone's daughter, cousin, friend, or relative? Who are you when you're standing on your own?

Being alone may feel awkward at first, but it can be a chance to give yourself the opportunity to listen to your own voice (and maybe God's, too). For many of us, it may be the first time we have ever done that. As with everything new, we get better at it with practice, and it becomes easier to accept.

CHAPTER 6

Alone in a Crowd

"Water, water everywhere / Nor any drop to drink."
— Samuel Taylor Coleridge, "The Rime of the
Ancient Mariner"

M y Aunt Rita was unlike anyone I knew. She was a successful businesswoman who had never married or had children. Instead of a rambling ranch-style home littered with children's toys, she lived in a funky bungalow a short stroll from the beach. She wore dazzling jewelry and fashionable clothes, and laughed loudly. All of that made her wonderful to my teenage sensibilities, but it wasn't what made her an enigma. The riddle, the part teenage me couldn't understand, was how comfortable she was being by herself. She took solo vacations and even went out to eat alone. Mind-blowingly, she didn't even feel the need to bring along with her a book to read. I've never known another person who was so comfortable with the quiet that comes from being the only person in a room, or one so at ease being by herself in a crowd.

I lived with my aunt for a short time when I was a teenager. I learned from her example that a person who genuinely likes herself doesn't need the approval of others, and that whether or not you are happy and content with where you are in life is a choice you make. I went to parties with her and saw a woman who didn't need to be the most popular girl in the room, the center of attention, who considered an evening a success if she had even one good conversation. Her example taught me the power of patience, good questions, and an interest in other people in navigating through nearly any social situation.

When I moved to Oklahoma for college, I thought a lot about how my aunt lived. I tried to reach her contented ideal, but it was a stretch for me, especially since I'm an extrovert. Living fourteen hours away from home in an unfamiliar city, I ended up spending a lot of time alone in my quiet apartment that fall. I discovered that I need noise and life around me, so I got a dog. Gala was a great companion at home, but I wasn't finding much in the way of friends anywhere near my age. At nineteen years old, my closest companion was the forty-five-year-old, three-times-divorced woman I worked with, whose only son was in prison. (My mother was thrilled.)

My boyfriend dragged me to house parties and get-togethers with his friends, but their tight-knit clique wasn't exactly recruiting new members. I went to parties and sat off to the side, holding the beer I would inevitably be handed. (I've never been a fan of beer, but holding it made me feel so grown-up.) I sat on couches in an ever-changing litany of living rooms and learned about loneliness. I learned especially that being lonely doesn't always mean being literally alone, because I was rarely by myself.

Being lonely in those crowded spaces came from being isolated and without social support. In my mind, I was invisible to the people around me, and I knew that even if I had set myself on fire, no one would have paid much more attention to my being there. We had no connection. I was, as my grandmother would call it, a wallflower. I was scenery in the background of what was going on. Most importantly, I sat there being scenery to myself. Even I didn't think I was important enough to talk to, and I talk to myself all the time, so you know it was a sad situation. There were people all around me, and I was still dying of loneliness.

Twenty-something years later, awkward parties are a whole new story. My husband (the same boyfriend from all those years ago) still takes me to gatherings I would never venture to on my own. These days we're not hanging with his childhood friends, but with his favorite collection of IT computer nerds. There are whole evenings that pass without anyone speaking a language that sounds remotely like English (they all speak their own brand of computerese). I'm not fluent in nerdspeak, so mostly I smile and listen. If anyone asks my opinion, I say, "If it's giving you problems, try turning it off, counting to three, and then turning it back on again," which is everything about technology that I've learned in twenty-plus years of marriage to a computer guru. I tease him that on these evenings I'm there as his emotional-support animal — I'm cute and it makes him happy to have me around. He smiles because it's true, but also because he loves me.

It's easy in a group like this, where I'm obviously the odd man out, to just let them talk while my mind wanders. I don't fit in, and they don't know me; plus I know that the main attraction is my husband. It would all be so easy if only I didn't know better. Every female relation I have has drilled into my head that a guest has an obligation at a gathering to help the event be a success. (We're Southern, and I went to finishing school. Miss Manners is almost a religion around my house.) The host needs to be welcoming and have things planned to go smoothly, so you have the duty to be more than a bump on a log, no matter how out of place you feel.

There are a couple of ways to approach that "alone in a crowd" feeling, no matter where you are — church, a party, a work function, or even hanging out at the neighborhood pool. (A moment of respect for those of us who manage to be brave and friendly while wearing a swimsuit.)

Find one good conversation and hunker down

There are few things better than going someplace where you don't know anybody and ending up having one of the best conversations of your life. Every person you meet has a story to tell or something you can learn from them, and most people are just waiting for a willing audience to listen to their tale. If you play your cards right, they'll tell it to you.

I once spent an entire evening at a wedding reception for some distant relative, listening to another guest regale me with the tale of her romantic evening with Elvis's ghost. I can't swear that the story she told me was true, but it was the funniest thing I'd heard in a long time. She was a perfectly ordinary-looking woman who just happened to be seated at our table. I asked her what was the most amazing thing that had ever happened to her, and she was off and running with her story about the rock legend's poltergeist.

You really never know what you're going to get, but think of all the stories you wouldn't hear if you didn't give other people the chance to tell you theirs.

Focus the attention on someone else

Focusing the spotlight determinedly on someone else is one of the best ways I've found to get over myself. I'm not talking about fawning fan-girl goobery, but about really paying attention to people and what they have to say. Listening for what someone says and listening just to respond are very different things. If I'm flying solo, I look for a person who looks like the odd man out and become her wingman for the evening whenever I can. It's so easy to do if you ask good questions and really listen to the answers. I ask about their families, their hobbies, their opinions on all kinds of things, and about the adventures they've had in their lives. Then I give them all the time they need to respond. Then, at the first opportunity, I introduce the person I'm with to the next person to come along, pointing out all the amazing things I've learned. Do this once, and you've made someone's night. Do it over and over for everyone you meet, and you'll not only be invited back; you'll be too busy to be alone.

People-watching and making small talk

When my mood is chill, the group is large, and I am not there for a purpose — that is, it's not a work function — I'll spend an evening on the periphery, making small talk with anyone who wanders my way, but mostly I like people-watching, or enjoying the food or entertainment. If you're on your own, you tend to notice things you'd otherwise have missed in a crowd.

No matter what strategy helps you cope with being alone in a crowd, there are ultimately two paths: One is to meet other people, strike up a conversation, and become a part of the group around you. The other is the ultimate solution, which is to be comfortable enough with yourself that being by yourself is a comfortable place to be.

CHAPTER 7

Be Yourself, Not an Impostor

*"Remember always that you not only have the right to be an
individual, you have an obligation to be one."*
— Eleanor Roosevelt

The house my husband grew up in was warm and
welcoming with a very traditional feel to it. My mother-
in-law has decorated her home with cobalt-blue glass, pictures
she needlepointed, and a kitchen filled with watermelon
accents. It's not at all what I would choose for my own home,
but it's absolute perfection for hers.

When Ben and I were newlyweds, his parents made no
effort to hide their bewilderment that he had chosen to marry
me. I was the antithesis of the life they knew and cherished.
They were quiet, and I was loud. Their lives were sure and
steady, while mine was an ever-expanding ball of chaos. I
was not the fairy-tale princess they had dreamed of for their
beloved son, and I was keenly aware of that fact.

At the time, I wanted nothing more than to fit neatly into
their Norman Rockwellesque family. They were all-American,
apple pie people, and I tried to cram myself into their mold.
Instead of my mother-in-law's watermelons, I filled my kitchen
shelves with the birdhouses she called "charming" and put blue
and yellow flowers all over my house. I consciously mimicked
their family's traditions, taking careful note of the recipes my

husband's parents liked best. In my quest to be accepted, I abandoned my vocal agnosticism to sit in the pew beside his grandparents every Sunday morning. I don't know what they were praying for, but I was praying that they would somehow learn to like me.

The harder I tried, the less they trusted me. It was probably because the image I was working so hard to portray was a lie, and they could smell it. In reality, all my hard work didn't make me fit in any better. It made his family wonder how Ben could have fallen in love with and married someone who was so clearly hiding something. And I was. I was hiding me.

The charade became exhausting, of course. After a few months, I admitted to myself that it wasn't working, and I gave it up. What was the point of trying so hard to fit in with people who didn't want me in their tribe? Then a funny thing happened. Once I stopped trying to be the person I thought they wanted, and just became myself — quirky eccentricities and all — the relationships with my in-laws became easier. It wasn't me that they'd objected to, but that I wasn't being honest about who I was. Instead of sticking out awkwardly, I finally found my own place at the table.

My mother-in-law may not choose to decorate her own surroundings with the same colorful abandon that I love, but she has learned to appreciate it, and me along with it. On a shopping trip last fall, during which I purchased a rainbow-colored rhinestone-encrusted iguana-shaped ring, she hugged me and laughed: "You are such a gift to all of us. You're here to save us from the color beige." I like to think that she's right about that, and that I only had to be myself for us both to figure it out.

"Just be yourself" sounds like such a simple thing to do. In reality it's not easy at all. What if the person you are is a huge jerk? What if you show the world who you really are and no one likes what they see? That's the big fear, isn't it? It's the fear of rejection that makes us hide behind an assumed persona and sometimes choose to act like an idiot, if that's what it takes to protect our hearts.

Many of us have been hiding for so long that we no longer know who we are, but we can't expect to find our people until we've peeled back those onion layers to find our authentic selves. It will be once we know who we are that we can figure out what kind of people we want and need around us. The problem with embarking on a journey of self-discovery is that it can get pretty lonely and sometimes take us to an unhealthy place of self-absorption. It's a catch-22 — we need to know who we are to find the people we need, but we need people around us to help us figure out who we are and keep us grounded. Maybe we need to start somewhere simpler.

Be genuine

What if instead of "be yourself" we told ourselves to "be genuine"? To be genuine means to allow our words and actions to be rooted unapologetically in our personalities, beliefs, values, gifts, and limitations, the things we most hope to be accepted for. That doesn't mean we have to go around telling everyone we meet exactly what we think, or fully exploit every opportunity to "express ourselves." It's more along the lines of the quote often attributed to Saint Francis of Assisi: "Preach the Gospel at all times. When necessary, use words." If we let our beliefs and values influence and guide the ways we interact with the world, we won't need to go around telling others everything we know. People will know who we are simply by meeting us.

Being genuine does not mean treating everyone exactly the same. We know this instinctively. We will, of course, treat our grandmothers differently than we treat a stranger who is behind us in line at the grocery store. We behave one way with our children and a different way with the creepy guy who lives next door. There's nothing wrong or hypocritical in treating people differently, as long as we don't contradict ourselves by communicating one version of ourselves to one person and the opposite to another.

A genuine approach to being ourselves is living in a way that is a true reflection of our beliefs, values, and truth. It means we can be unashamed of our opinions, but at the same time respectful of everyone else's. It means interacting with other people in ways that are relatable and appropriate to the situation. That sounds good, right? But what does it look like in the real world?

Don't compare yourself with others

When our own lives don't feel as if they are going exactly according to the scripts in our heads, it's tempting to look around and judge what we have going on against everyone else's measuring stick. Instagram and Facebook are filled with smiling faces, perfect families, and grand adventures. The thing about those Pinterest-worthy images is that they're often lies. The images of perfection are rarely spontaneous snapshots of real life. They are posed, planned, and set up for the camera. They're also filtered, cropped, and tweaked in order to show off the very best possible images of the stories they want to tell.

It's important to keep in mind that while we're wearing old sweats, munching barbeque chips, and feeling as though we don't measure up to other people's standards, they don't really measure up to those imaginary standards either. We're all hot messes in our own ways, so we need to stop comparing the unedited, inside view of our own lives with other people's exterior, crafted images of perfection. It's all an illusion. Don't fall into the trap of comparing yourself with who you imagine other people to be. Let go of worrying about what anyone else thinks of you. Their opinions are their business, not yours. You don't have a right to what they think, and you probably don't really want to know anyway.

Listen to your gut

Figure out what you do and don't like, what you can and can't tolerate, and what you would avoid an any cost. Decide what your nonnegotiables are in friendships, and stick to your guns. While friendship should push us out of our comfort zones every now and again, it shouldn't ask us to do anything we are truly uncomfortable doing or witnessing. We all have an internal alarm that goes off when what's going on is questionable, and we need to listen to that inner voice.

People who are worth the time and effort will respect our commitment to live according to our own code of ethics. If someone isn't willing or able to see that each person is a unique individual with a distinct personality, shake the dust from your sandals and walk on.

Find things you like doing and then do them

What are the things you enjoy in life? What kinds of things fill your bucket list? Do you dream of traveling to far-off locations, perhaps walking the Camino someday or attending Mass in the Catacombs? Is your idea of a perfect afternoon one spent snuggled under the covers with a good book, or would you rather spend the day at the gym lifting weights and racing a clock until the sweat drips from your exhausted self? Whatever it is that gets your heart racing and brings a smile to your face, as long as it's not going to get you into trouble in this world or the next, then do it! Don't wait for anyone else to tag along. Just put on your cosplay costume or your ballet shoes and go.

Our preferences are just as valid as anyone else's, but no one will know what they are if we don't speak up. Eat the foods you like and say no thank you to the ones you don't. Have the extra slice of pie. It's okay to avoid the creepy uncle's house at Christmas and opt for Midnight Mass instead as long as you are honest about what's going on. That doesn't mean you should be brutal with the truth or wield it like a weapon. There are ways of saying things that soften the blow. If you can't figure out how, take a cue from those of us in the Deep South and add "Bless his heart" to the end of whatever you say. (It erases a multitude of hurt feelings down here, and your mama will talk to you about those it doesn't later.)

It's easy to put the things that make us happy on hold in an effort to satisfy the hopes and dreams of the people we love. There's nothing wrong with making their dreams important, as long as we don't forget that we have things we dream of as well.

CHAPTER 8

Family Issues

*"Sometimes the best we can do is to remind each other that
we're related for better or for worse ... and try to keep the
maiming and killing to a minimum."*
— Rick Riordan, *Sea of Monsters*

There are people in this world who have been gifted with intact, healthy, and loving families. Still others have families that are slightly dysfunctional and wildly eccentric. Others have families that are broken or blended, cobbled together by the unshakable bonds of "there's no one else I'd rather be with." Some of us have none of the above, and our families look more like a "Choose Your Own Adventure" book than any kind of discernible family tree. We all have to come from somewhere, even if we don't know exactly how to describe what it is.

My husband grew up in the kind of family that Norman Rockwell dreamed about — grandparents across the street, aunts and cousins around the corner, kids running in and out and welcome anywhere they went. It's more than just a 1950s daydream; it's the way we would all be living if the world were perfect. Human beings are herd animals (you did read the introduction, didn't you?), which means that we're designed to want to be near our families, safe and loved. (Again, in a perfect world that happens. Sadly, this world isn't perfect.)

Until very recently in human history, families lived in a multigenerational setup. People expected to live with a grandma, their mother-in-law, and a spinster aunt or two, plus their own kids all in the same household. People were all up in each other's chili, and it was normal. There were a lot of hands to help with the children, and a lot of opinions about how to raise them (which isn't necessarily a bad thing). While it's no longer the way most people live in Western societies, it does still exist here and there. It's the chupacabra of families, talked about a lot, but not often seen in the bright light of day; it's a way of life that's sadly disappearing.

We were designed to need family structures, but the reality for many of us is that that is a thing of the past. Part of this is because society has become more mobile, with families moving for jobs, education, or even on a whim much more than they used to. Once we all started moving around, the tight-knit families that were our safety nets and cultural touchstones began to disintegrate and disappear. There are other, much deeper, factors contributing to the disintegration of families, of course, but those are outside the scope of this book. The point is, lots of us don't have strong families, and reports of loneliness and depression are skyrocketing. We need a tribe, and without one we wander through life a little bit lost.

There are people like my husband who have been blessed with an amazing, or at least functioning, family of origin. If that's you, you should do whatever it takes to maintain those bonds. Live nearby and be an active part of each other's lives if that's possible. Find ways to stay in touch, travel to see each other whenever you can, and be part of the life of your family. Other people dream about what you have. Some spend a small fortune on sites like 23andMe to dig up their roots because they want so badly to belong.

The good news: If your family of origin looks a little more mishmash than apple pie perfection, you can still have the family that you dream of, but you're going to have to collect them for yourself.

We lost many of my mom's gifts to a traumatic brain injury

(TBI) when I was fourteen. She is the first person who would tell you that she isn't the same woman she was. She's also quick to point out that I'm not the girl I was either. It's a fair point. While my mom may have survived the car crash, our family didn't. Mom had been the glue that held her side of our large extended family together. She may have been the baby, but she was also their bedrock, the touchstone they all depended upon. When she changed, they all drifted off into their own lives, and our family never recovered.

A few years later, my father moved out and divorced her. He chose to begin his own life anew rather than to live in the constant turmoil that is the aftermath of a TBI. Within a few years, he married again, gaining not only a new wife, but also new children. As too often happens with divorced families, he eventually became wholly a part of that new family, and abdicated his position in ours.

The complete disintegration of our family happened very quickly. My mom was frightening to be around. My brothers' and my emotional needs were overwhelming, so the people we depended on walked away. Where we had once been a part of a too-many-people-to-fit-in-the-house-at-Thanksgiving family, it was suddenly just us — and then just me. In a flurry of hurt and anger, I left the Church and turned my back on God.

When I found the courage to return to the Church in my mid-twenties, I stopped wishing for just any family to belong to and started praying for a Catholic one. Though I had fallen in love with my Catholic faith, I didn't really have any idea what it looked like to live a Catholic life. I daydreamed about having Catholic grandparents for my children, but didn't see how such a thing could be possible. As it turned out, that didn't matter. God knew the desire of my heart, and in him there is always a way.

Across town from us lived an older couple whose children had joined the military, left the Church, and moved far away. They prayed nightly Rosaries for their children to return to the faith and for their grandchildren to be raised Catholic, but God didn't seem to be in a hurry to answer their prayers. They were complete strangers to us when we sat behind them on a Sunday morning in August 2001. Our third baby, Lincoln, was, at two weeks old, a sweet boy with duck-fluff hair and loud opinions. Mass had just begun when he began loudly complaining about the music. The more I tried to shush him, the louder his fretting and fuss became. Tears were prickling the back of my eyes. Two babies had been doable, but three was already overwhelming. Right before the tears began to fall, the woman sitting in front of us turned around.

With a mischievous smile, she lifted my red-faced newborn right out of my arms. It didn't even occur to me to object. "Come and see your Oma," she crooned softly. He sighed deeply, closed his eyes, and sank into her arms. He knew her from the first moment she held him. "Look, Opa," she said to her husband. "Look at this beautiful naughty boy."

"Hey, there," he whispered to my son. "There's no need to holler. You're with your Oma now." And with that he traced a cross on my son's forehead with his thumb and whispered a blessing over him. They have been our family's beloved Oma and Opa ever since.

I can't explain what kind of alchemy made them my parents or me their daughter. I just know that one day they were. I was a grown woman in my late twenties when we met on that summer Sunday, but by Christmas they had become the parents I had wished for since I was a teenager. As we curled up on the couch watching the children open presents, Opa put his arm around me and pulled me into one of his famous bear hugs. "We sure love you, kid," he said. "Me and Ma, we're so lucky to have found a rotten kid like you." I kissed his cheek and laid my head upon his shoulder, beyond lucky to be his girl.

I learned from Oma and Opa, and from my husband's relatives, what it took to have a healthy extended family. Over the years we've added to our little clan friends and neighbors who became siblings, aunts, uncles, and cousins. While our family may not be related to us by blood, they are the one we're lucky to have.

Whether your family is held together by genetics or by choice, there are some common traits that help keep families close and make sure that "the ties that bind" are double-knotted:

Have a sense of humor

"You can get away with almost anything if it makes Mom laugh," my children will whisper to each other when they know they're in trouble, and most of the time it's true. Life with this many people living under the same roof, and a large extended family not living under my roof (thank goodness), inevitably leads to conflicts of personality, points of view, or just plain squabbling over "but the red cup is m-m-m-m-m-i-i-i-i-i-i-i-n-n-n-n-e."

Laughter deflates a lot of awkwardness and skims over the rough spots. Inside jokes and private jokes (that aren't cruel or mean) are part of what make a family "us." Matchmaking relatives, nagging grandmothers, the one perfect cousin you're always compared with, and questions you'd rather not answer can all be deflected with a good belly laugh.

Life is funny, and family should be, too. A silly joke that's been told a hundred times may be the only common ground you have on which to build relationships, but it's a toehold, and sometimes that's all you need.

Speak the truth in charity

We all have things we'd rather not say out loud, and it can be tempting to gild the lily or even to lie once in a while. In addition to putting you smack dab in line for the confessional, you're sure to be found out sooner or later. No one will be onto the truth of your life faster than the people who raised you. They've seen the way you blush; they know your eye twitches when you're lying, and that you can't look Mama in the eye when you're fibbing. Your family has been watching your tics since you were a bitty little thing, so don't even try it.

Honesty is the best way to build relationships with friends and relatives. They want to know and love the real you, so you should share that with them. If they could live through the years of your decorating furniture with Sharpies and cutting off your baby sister's ponytail, they can weather whatever storm you've got going on in your life if you give them the chance.

The truth, however, doesn't have to be as raw as a slap in the face. Your cousin may not be as friendly with his deodorant as perhaps he should be, but there are gentle ways to say that as well as cruel ones. When you get the opportunity to be kind, you won't regret taking it.

We teach our children that before they speak they should ask themselves, "Is what I'm saying true? Is it necessary? Is it kind?" and that the answer to all three should be yes. It's a pretty good rule for life.

Spend time together

"You need to spend time together" seems like such an obvious thing to say, and yet it becomes more difficult all the time. It's nearly impossible to have a meaningful relationship with people you don't spend any time with. You can hold fond memories of them, but eventually the relationship begins to fall away.

If I could wave my magic wand, we would spend every Sunday with our families, swapping stories and chowing down on Grandma's pot roast and mashed potatoes. Our lives would weave around one another, and our relationships would be ongoing. If you have that kind of family, I'm more than a little jealous of you. Soak up the time at home whenever you can.

For those of us who live more than a short drive away, it takes an effort to stay close, but it's worth the extra work. Stay in touch with regular phone calls or Skyping. I know texting is easier, but it's also less personal, and no substitute for the sound of your favorite aunt's voice. Call if you have to, but go home when you can. Death is a sad fact of life, and one we prefer not to think about, but our relatives won't be around forever, no matter how invincible they've always seemed. Go wrap your grandma in a hug, take your dad fishing, or just sit and listen to the tales of generations past. Time with the people who love you is time well spent. That way your mom's face lights up when you walk through the door? You should make that happen as many times in your life as you possibly can.

Love unconditionally, but have high hopes

My mother used to tell me, "I love you forever, no matter what," then she'd kiss my forehead and whisper, "Be amazing." I would laugh and ask her what she meant: that she loved me no matter what or that I should be amazing no matter what? When I succeeded, she jumped up and down in wild celebration, and when I failed miserably, she was the comfort I wanted most of all.

Families love us through the hills and the valleys of our lives. It's a cradle-to-grave operation. More often than not, their dreams for what we can achieve eclipse our own. Whether they are ours from birth or sometime after that, good families accept us for the people we are today, and have hopes of even better for who we will be tomorrow.

"I have big plans for you," Oma tells my children. "You're all going to be saints someday."

"What if I'm not?" one of my boys asked her.

"Then we'll pray you into heaven. That's what families do."

I don't know that it's possible to hope and love any better than that.

If your family is unhealthy, abusive, or unsafe for any reason, shake the dust from your sandals and walk away. There are people out there in the world who will be excited to love you and add you to their clan. Let them. You have a right to be mentally and emotionally healthy. There is no guilt in going in search of where you belong.

CHAPTER 9

Friendship Issues

"It takes a great deal of bravery to stand up to our enemies, but just as much to stand up to our friends."
— J. K. Rowling, *Harry Potter and the Sorcerer's Stone*

It's astounding how quickly problems can arise in even the best friendships. One moment you're skipping along the yellow brick road together — snatching apples from talking trees, singing and dancing a little, looking amazing in your ruby slippers. And then — BOOM! — out of nowhere come the flying monkeys. Things can change at a whiplash pace as a person you love becomes someone you wonder why you like — or even someone you aren't convinced still likes you.

Friendships become difficult when people aren't open and honest with each other and communication breaks down between the two of you. Throw in a healthy dose of selfishness, and you've got a perfect recipe for friendship disaster. In a perfect world, all friendships would be "other focused," with each friend prioritizing the other's needs above her own. Everyone gets taken care of that way. But in this fallen and broken world, it's very easy to slip away from the ideal and wonder, "What's in it for me?"

Looking out for our own needs is part of human nature — the part that keeps us from starving to death. Placing the needs of people who aren't relatives above or even on par with our own goes against our baser instincts. Just because it's hard, however, doesn't mean that we get a pass for selfish behavior. It simply means that a "me first" attitude is something we all have to acknowledge, struggle against, and strive to overcome.

It's not hard to fix the rough patches in a relationship when you know they're there, but what if you don't? Here are some red flags to look for, not just in your friends, but in yourself.

The collector of wrongs

I once had a very dear friend who was a collector of wrongs. She never told people when they crossed a line or hurt her feelings; she just held on to hurt and resentment. I suppose that she kept hoping her friends would figure out that she was unhappy and do something about it. She gave no obvious indications that anything was wrong until she got to the point of exploding in anger. She would suddenly rage in her friends' stunned faces, burning bridges and considering herself better off without such horrible and insensitive friends around her. But were they really such horrible friends to begin with? Or were they simply treating her the way she had taught them was acceptable?

In her desire to avoid conflict and not ruffle any feathers, she drove off friend after friend. Many of those relationships had the potential of being really good ones, if only she had been honest instead of keeping a collection of all the wrongs she had suffered. People can't fix what they don't know is wrong. Either tell them what's going on, or let it go. Completely. Anything else is unfair.

The silent treatment

Almost as frustrating as a collector of wrongs is a friend who uses the silent treatment. In my opinion, the silent treatment is only appropriate when you're five years old. It's right up there with holding your breath until you get your way. Avoiding conversation with a friend while you're angry so that you don't say something you may later regret can be a good idea as long as you let her know what's going on.

"I'm really mad right now, and I want to talk about it, but

I need to calm down a bit first" is a perfectly fine thing to say. And if you're the person who gets told that, you need to respect your friend's request for time and not push to talk right this minute. But you do have to talk eventually, even if it's just to say goodbye.

If it is your friend who's giving you the cold and silent treatment, and you're sure there's not something going on in her life that's sucking up her attention, ask for an explanation. But if she's still silent, then give her a little breathing room. It's either a genuine attempt at trying to find space and clarity, or it's a tantrum. If she's just looking for time and perspective on how to deal with the wonder that is you, let her take all the time that she needs. If it's a tantrum to let you know just how hurt and angry the pouty baby is, you've got some serious thinking to do, such as, "Do I want to be friends with someone who throws kindergarten temper tantrums instead of putting on her big-girl panties and just dealing?" Well, do you?

If you are the person who uses the silent treatment to make a point, it's time to stop. Emotional manipulation is not ever acceptable or kind, and the silent treatment is the epitome of emotional manipulation. Stop playing games and just talk about what's going on. Everyone you know will thank you for it.

Intermediaries

Also not fun are the friends who won't deal with anything directly but prefer to go through an intermediary. "Can you tell Rebecca that she was rude when she ... " No. Just no. It doesn't matter how big your clutch of friends is, all relationships are one-on-one. Intermediaries actually help only a tiny handful of times. More often than not, anyone willing to jump into the middle of conflict between friends is a pot stirrer or a drama junkie. Their need or desire to be in the middle of the excitement isn't going to help anyone settle anything. Kick them out of the in between. If someone is your friend, then you should be able to talk things over without relying on a referee.

If you really are afraid of her, or she's afraid of you, then you're not really friends, and you probably don't want to be.

As long as you and your friends can talk honestly and openly about your relationship, you're going to be fine. Every relationship hits rocky ground now and again. Rough patches don't have to mean the end of a friendship. They can be opportunities for you both to grow as individuals as well as for your friendship to mature.

If, however, you keep having the same problems over and over again with different friends, there may be something deeper to it, and that something might be you. If your friendships all seem to end the same way, with the same kinds of arguments and complaints, it could be that you are the toxic person in the mix. Go and talk to someone. There is no shame in needing either (or both) spiritual or psychiatric help. You may find that friendships are easier to find and maintain if you're starting from a place of good mental health.

CHAPTER 10

What Are You Willing to Invest?

"I learned that a real friendship is not about
what you can get, but about what you can give.
Real friendship is about making sacrifices and investing in
people to help them improve their lives."
— Eric Thomas, *The Secret to Success*

The scope of things we can learn these days is limited only by human imagination. There are classes for parenting, beekeeping, sports, glass blowing, and a dizzying number of other options about which we can learn, thereby filling our days and giving meaning and direction to our lives. Sometimes, we think these kinds of skills are so important that we sacrifice in other areas of our lives in order to make them possible, for our children and/or ourselves. With all this energy being expended on "life enrichment" activities, I wonder why we don't spend more time teaching and learning about how to maintain relationships, which truly add meaning to our lives?

Friendships are rooted in moments of "soul validation." You're standing in a coffee shop surrounded by strangers, and the woman in front of you orders an obnoxious "large, half-whole milk, one-quarter 1 percent, one-quarter nonfat, extra hot, split quad shots, no foam latte, with whip, two Splendas, one sugar in the raw, one pump of vanilla, three short sprinkles of cinnamon, upside down," and you lock eyes with the barista in a mutual look of "what the actual heck." In that moment, the two of you are in complete sync. That's the validation. You're instantly on the same side of the issue and two seconds from an "I feel you" fist-pump salute. A great friendship can grow from a moment like that. Or, you may just have found a favorite barista and become her newest favorite customer ever. (That's not a bad thing.)

That instant moment of recognition, the spark of connection, can only get you so far in the search for your people. Whether you've had a friendship spark with the barista or your next-door neighbor, even love-at-first-sight friendships take time to develop. Even if your gut tells you that this human being is going to be a part of your life for the rest of your days, you cannot force intimacy, and you will not have a deep and abiding bond within moments. It takes effort for a friendship to last longer than the first excited flush of getting to know you. Creating a relationship is like baking a soufflé; if you push too hard and skip the necessary bits, it's going to collapse.

The old cliché holds true — if you're going to have a friend, you are going to have to be a friend. The saying has been around for so long because there's so much truth in it. But what does it really mean? What it's all going to come down to is one word — investment. At forty-three years old, I'm keenly aware that, from an actuarial point of view, I'm about halfway through my life. Every moment is precious and sacred. The time I spend with my friends is time borrowed from my family. Time is something I am happy to share with my friends, but I want to make darn sure it's an investment that is worth my effort.

You don't have to be middle-aged before you learn how incredibly valuable your time is, but it certainly is easier to see. There are questions that you will need to answer. How much of yourself are you willing to pour into the life and well-being of the other person, and how much is she willing to pour into yours? And how much does each of you need from a friend?

Get on the same page

The Bible warns about being unequally yoked, or mismatched, to your spouse in matters of faith (see 2 Cor 7:13–14). I'm here to tell you that it's the same in all aspects of any relationship. If one of you does the heavy lifting and the other is phoning it in, you're out of balance. The one of you doing all the work is eventually going to get tired of it and burn out. She's going to be drained dry and have nothing left to give. That dry-husk relationship is just going to shrivel up and blow away, and resentment is likely to take its place.

Of course, any relationship is going to require you to stretch your boundaries a little bit; a little growth and compromise is good for you. Life would be boring if we were all the same; so would friendship. Friends have to be on the same page about what this commitment is going to look like. There may need to be a DTR (define the relationship) conversation, or merely a need to feel each other out. But for goodness sakes, be honest with each other if you're feeling smothered by a clingy friend, or left out in the cold by someone who may not naturally need as much attention as you do.

We all come to new relationships lugging old baggage from the life that has come before. Sometimes that emotional suitcase is pretty light, but other times it's so heavy that you absolutely need it to be a bag on wheels. Either way, own that. Be upfront about your daddy issues and fear of abandonment. (That's not just me, right?) But don't wallow in it. That way, when your life goes a bit sideways, you can just say: "Sorry, daddy issues. Remember?" Anyone who is willing to fess up to the kind of cross he is carrying is worth the time and effort it takes to forge a friendship. On the other hand, someone who has blinders on and either doesn't see or won't admit where his wounds are will be difficult to be close with over time.

Shakespeare wrote: "All the world's a stage, and all the men and women merely players.... One man in his time plays many parts." What Shakespeare said about our place in the world also holds true for relationships. We all have roles that we naturally fulfill; it's the way our puzzles fit together. Who we are to each other isn't intentional; it's organic. We become caretakers, the voice of reason, the consoler, the cheerleader, naturally. In a healthy relationship, our roles change and evolve. We may even switch it up completely when the occasion calls for it. What happens, though, when you don't see your place in the relationship the way your counterpart does?

For eleven years, my closest friend in the world was a military wife who had lived down the street from our family for a handful of years. We had loved each other through deployments, infertility, surprise babies, and the painful lack of sleep and usage of brain cells that accompanies new motherhood. She regularly touted her Ivy League education and New England pedigree, and I would laugh because those things didn't matter in the flat plains of Oklahoma. I was more impressed by the woman than by her labels, and saw us as equals. She, however, was slightly older than I was and saw herself as my mentor. We both talked about our mutual love of writing: me with my blog and her with the novel she was forever thinking of writing.

This mismatch in our perceptions of who we were wasn't an impediment until the summer that I published my first book. Hers was still in the talking-about-it stage. Suddenly our roles flipped, and I was the one with more experience. My accomplishment upset the balance of our relationship, and it never recovered. We were too entrenched in our "places" for us to make the transition.

What killed our relationship began with our roles and ended with our egos.

When our identities are wrapped up in what we perceive our places to be, it can be shattering to have that position ripped away from us. Such a drastic redefinition is survivable, but it comes back to the question of investment. Both friends have to be willing to invest the necessary effort to survive growing pains. And when they're done, both friends need to adapt and figure out who they are in the relationship over and over again. Relationships aren't static, thank goodness — they live, grow, and change over a lifetime.

Whether it's conscious or not, in the beginning of relationships there are rules on which you mutually agree. Do you call each other every day, or are you texters? Is weekly phone contact enough, or do you need to lay eyes on each other more often than that? Are you the kinds of friends who talk about everything, or are there things you prefer to keep private? Each friendship is unique and will go along according to its own playbook, until the relationship becomes deeper than the rules. When the person who hates unexpected guests suddenly leaves her front door unlocked so that you can walk in at any time without knocking, when the person who prickles at criticism can be told "you're a witch today" and have it accepted with an acknowledgment and an apology instead of offense, when two famous talkers find that words aren't necessary and they can enjoy sitting in silence with each other, that's the Holy Grail of friendship. If you've got that, it's precious and rare, and you should make sure to invest deeply, because this one is worth it.

CHAPTER 11

Personality Types

*"It's no use going back to yesterday.
I was a different person then."*
— Lewis Carroll, *Alice in Wonderland*

We like to assign ourselves labels, to declare ourselves native members of one tribe or another. A lot of us don't think twice about making an effort to figure out who we are and why we do the wacky things we do. We toss around the alphabet soup of the Myers-Briggs personality test as though four letters could provide the Rosetta stone for understanding one another. "I'm an INTJ, and she's an ENFP, so you know what that means ... " (Most people don't actually know what that means, because we haven't bothered to memorize all of the possible combinations. But we nod along as if we do.) It's the friend-seekers' version of Garanimals — those kids' clothes that tell you your outfit works because they have the same picture on the labels.

It would be convenient if friendship worked that way: "I have a lion tag and you have a lion tag, so let's be friends." Fortunately, or unfortunately depending on how you see it, people are much too complex to be completely defined by an animal tag or a four-letter label. In reality, it takes a lifetime to understand what makes another person tick. Still, those

Myers-Briggs letters are a good starting place, especially the first ones — the I or the E.

If you spend any time at all looking around the internet, it can sometimes seem as though the world is split into two separate tribes — introverts and extroverts. The brilliant but reclusive introverts, the memes tell us, crave a world of calm and quiet, spending their days reading, writing poetry, thinking deep thoughts, and being made uncomfortable by the loudness of their extrovert counterparts. Extroverts, on the other hand, are the loud jocks and class clowns of the world — friendly and gregarious, a little on the dumb side, and unable to spend a single moment without their posse by their sides. In short, the life of every toga party. If you've ever worn a crown in public and you're not actually royalty, chances are you're an extrovert.

These two imaginary tribes of polar opposites living in two separate worlds filled with paths that never cross don't really exist at all. Real people can't be so perfectly and neatly divided. Real people tend to be a lot messier than that. But while these preferences help to make up our personalities and our approaches toward friendship, they are not set in stone. Most people will slide about on the scale between social butterfly and absolute recluse throughout their lifetimes. It's helpful to understand the tendencies toward introversion and extroversion. This information stops being helpful when the labels of introvert or extrovert become the excuse that you hide behind for not fully living your life.

A lot of frustration arises in friendships when we feel as though we're misunderstood, so let's take a look at this aspect of personality and see if we can't all just get along. With so much attention these days focused on the introverts among us, let's start with the party crowd.

Extroverts
Extroverts feed off their environment
It's a bit of a simplification to say that extroverts like people. They actually need them. Extroverted people feed off the

energy of those around them, recharging their batteries as they go. Does that mean that every extrovert likes loud and wild parties? Absolutely not.

The more, the merrier — two may be company, but three is better

As an extrovert, I'm never happier than when I have houseguests. I would have people over every weekend if I didn't think my husband would leave me. It's the perfect combination of having people nearby and not having to get out of my pajamas. Add in the fact that we don't have to stop talking because it's midnight, and I'm all in.

Pauses in conversation mean the other person is done talking

"I'm sorry, were you not done talking? You stopped to breathe, so I thought it was my turn again." My poor introvert husband has been interrupted and talked over since we started dating way back last century. It's yet another way that our brains function differently. He speaks in stops and starts, really thinking over what he wants to say long before the words are ever spoken. Thoughts come to my brain in a rush, and it can be extremely difficult to throw the brakes on them. He thinks I'm not listening and that I'm rudely interrupting. I'm just so happy to have a human being to talk to that I don't always stop to think much at all.

It may seem as if extroverts are all socially adept, loud, and friendly, but that's not necessarily true. We can be just as shy, awkward, and rude as anyone. The only thing that holds true for all of us is our need for community. Being alone will make us all slightly mad in the end. As for our "quieter" friends, the introverts, it turns out that they're not always so quiet after all.

Introverts
Sometimes they really do just want to be alone

Introverts can get overwhelmed and drained by constant

conversation and commotion. When he's had enough of all the people who refuse to go away and give him space, my husband says he's "touched out." At that point, he often disappears for hours at a time, usually into our bedroom with a book to read and headphones to cancel the noise.

There was a time when I thought his desire to be by himself had to mean that he was angry with me. Instead it meant that he was drained from the constant presence of people. He had paid the price for pushing himself through work and social situations, and now he needed to hide from the world and recharge his depleted batteries.

They think before they speak

Words are tools for introverts, and they like to use them purposefully. Where an extrovert can run over people and dominate a conversation, an introvert likes to take a little time to say exactly what he thinks. With an introvert, a pause is actually a pause and a sign of taking the conversation seriously.

They do like people, they just don't like crowds

There is a common misconception that introverts aren't social creatures, when they absolutely can be. "You hate everyone," I tease my husband all the time. He always replies: "That's not true. I like individuals just fine. It's people as a big group that I don't like." I know for a fact that he does like certain people. He finds them fascinating and would happily spend the better part of an evening in deep conversation — as long as that evening ended with everyone going to their own homes.

It's interesting to note that most of the duos you know, whether romantic or platonic, are a mix of introvert and extrovert. We are drawn to each other and seem to balance each other out.

For all the self-labeling we like to do, it turns out that people really are individuals. The labels can help us begin to understand each other, and personality is an interesting thing to study if you're so inclined. Love Languages, Four Temperaments, Myers-Briggs: all can contribute to how we reach out to others. No matter how accurate they are, however, they are no substitute for honest conversation and life experiences.

The point is, you can be friends with anyone. We're not Garanimals looking for perfect matches, but human beings looking for people to do life with. Often, the person who ends up being the best fit in the end wasn't the one who looked like a match on paper.

CHAPTER 12

So What if They Aren't Like You?

*"A friend is one that knows you as you are, understands
where you have been, accepts what you have become,
and still, gently allows you to grow."*
— William Shakespeare

When I was in elementary school, I was friends with everyone. Trivial matters like sex and race didn't matter. The things I considered important in potential friends were how far could they throw a football, how good their imaginations were, and whether they lived nearby. Our days were filled with mad games of make-believe and wild romps through the cornfields that ringed the neighborhood. Crybabies and tattletales weren't welcome, but everyone else was enthusiastically added to the game.

By the time I was thirty, my criteria had become more stringent. I no longer cared how far someone could heave a football, but I had developed a list of "nonnegotiables." As a result, I surrounded myself with women who were exactly like me — Catholic, home-schooling, big-family mamas. We were all cut from the same cloth and rarely challenged one another's points of view on the big family issues, but we would fight like demons over minutiae. We all believed that teaching our children at home was undoubtedly the best way to educate them, but squabbles over how to teach multiplication tables could turn into a death match. There was no need for any of us to stretch very far beyond our comfort zones. I was quite happy living in my perfectly constructed bubble until my husband's job relocated our family to Dallas, and I had to leave those carefully chosen friends behind.

We had been in Dallas only three weeks when my best friend from childhood reached out to me. A lot had changed in our lives since Mrs. Killian's class at St. Gertrude's School in our small Texas town. I had become an ultraconservative, pro-life, Catholic, home-schooling mom of eight; and Pat was now the liberal, feminist, lesbian, pro-choice, spiritual, hippieish mom of four. On paper, we were headed for a train wreck. In person, we were amazing together. Pat and I are solid proof that two people who seem to have nothing in common on the surface can find common ground and maintain a friendship that endures for years.

Now that I'm slightly older, I've given up on the ideal that all of my people will share all of my values, my opinions, and my point of view. It has meant learning to listen with the intention of understanding instead of listening to respond. The politically charged debates I loved when I was younger have given way to conversations seeking understanding. Some of my closest friendships are with people who don't look anything like me "on paper," and I've learned to enjoy the challenges that they bring as they push me beyond my assumptions. They require me to have a deeper understanding of what it is that I really do believe, and what I think is important. They've taught me not to write off anyone as a potential friend, because there are good and valuable friends to be found even in the unlikeliest of places.

My friends and I may come at life from totally different political, religious, and cultural views; yet somehow it manages to work. These friends each have qualities that I admire and ways I wish I were more like them. They each have characteristics that inspire me to examine and change myself for the better.

These kinds of relationships aren't always easy, and the

challenges they present are not for everyone or for every season of our lives. These kinds of friendships push us to examine all of the things that we profess to hold true, because we are going to get called to defend those positions more than once. In a healthy friendship, it looks a lot less like a UFC cage match and more like a deep and long running conversation of mutual respect. It flat-out won't work without mutual respect.

We form the deepest connections with those who strive to understand and accept us as human beings rather than as caricatures of religious/nonreligious stereotypes or political affiliations. It's impossible to be close to someone if you have to wear a mask, put on a persona, and keep your opinions to yourself. Friendship requires honesty and the security of knowing that you won't be attacked if you don't say all the "right words" or think all the "right thoughts."

Mutual interests are also essential. As different as you may look on paper, you have to have some common ground. Is it a love of cooking? Do you veg out to the same fandom? Do you share a secret and shameful love of Nickelback? Are your parenting philosophies more or less in sync? Do you both snort with laughter over the same inappropriate jokes? You need something light and easy to bond over, because life and friendship can't always be a deep and heavy philosophical exploration of each other's psyches.

As much work, patience, humility, and understanding as this kind of friendship requires, it comes with a huge upside. The first is the spice of variety. I can say from experience that while having all your friends look like you is easy, it can also be extremely boring. If you had the same bologna sandwich for lunch day in and day out, think how much you'd look forward to a nice turkey on rye once in a while. It's a palate cleanser, and not having to worry about fitting in can make a relationship feel a lot less pressured.

A friend who doesn't exactly mirror your own beliefs can be a relief, but she's also going to be the first one to call you out. Since she doesn't have a vested personal interest in the things you espouse, she's not going to be as willing to gloss over your inconsistencies or personal hypocrisies the same way someone who agrees with you will. In fact, your other friends may not even notice things this particular friend finds glaringly obvious.

Because your friend isn't sitting on the same soapbox you're on, getting a second opinion will really mean getting a different opinion, and that's a very good thing.

You don't only need someone who can parrot back to you what you think. You already know what you think. You may need someone who can look at things with fresh eyes. There's an old clichéd story about three blind men who encounter an elephant. One touches the trunk and thinks he's found a hose. The second runs his hands over the side of the elephant and declares that they've encountered a wall. The third feels the bristly tail and announces that this is surely a rope. It isn't until they combine the information from all three perspectives that they figure out they've been manhandling a pachyderm. That's the beauty of having an "opposite" friend. He can tell you the things you're missing by seeing things only from your point of view.

I have found that I am generally attracted to people who possess something I don't have — personality traits, knowledge, approach to life. I enjoy people with mindsets different from mine, not only for themselves, but also for the adventure and variety that they bring into my life. Our friendships are like long-running conversations that thankfully never end. We wear down the other's rough edges and learn to bring out the very best in each other. The loudly opinionated person learns to temper herself and make sure she communicates clearly, while the quiet friend learns to speak up and stand his ground. The perfectionist learns that mistakes are okay and differences are a gift. The narrow-minded sees the world in a new way and learns what it is that he truly believes.

It is in setting our cherished traditions and beliefs alongside the contrast of another that we can discern what is real, what is true, and what is beautiful. Another's strengths help our weaknesses — and we get to return the favor.

CHAPTER 13

In Praise of Our Virtual Friends

"the worst thing about online friendships is no hugs man i wanna hug the frick outta some of you"
— @bringinglexiback

I shushed the children and opened up my laptop, pulling up the livestream of St. Peter's Cathedral in Belfast, Northern Ireland, just in time to hear the good Father say: "The camera's up there. Everyone wave hello to the godmother." Leah's family all dutifully turned toward what I assume is the choir loft, smiled, and waved. I know they didn't see me, but I couldn't help but wave back. I beamed a proud godmother's smile from halfway around the world as I watched my beloved Naomi be welcomed into the Catholic faith.

I'd been praying for Naomi and her parents, Leah and Éamonn, ever since Leah had told me she was expecting. I was the first person who does not live in their house to know that this little Irish lass was on the way. I squealed with delight to know she was coming and was overflowed with emotion that her parents would trust me to be her godmother.

Naomi's mother and I have been friends for nearly fourteen years. We've chatted and prayed each other through some of the darkest times in each other's lives. It seems a bit odd to me that I could love someone so dearly whose voice I've only heard a handful of times and whose face I've never seen in real life.

It doesn't seem at all strange, however, that I'd be the godmother of a child whose parents I've never met. So much of my life is spent online that this seems completely normal to me. These days, most of my friends "live in my computer," as my five-year-old likes to say. Some of them I met in person first and then used the internet to maintain the relationship; others I met in various chat rooms, through blogging, or on social media. There is a natural inclination to think that these "virtual" friendships are, by their very nature, somehow less authentic than a relationship "in real life." I haven't found that to be true.

I hesitate to even divide my relationships into "online" and "off-line," as though one is less real or valuable than the other. The measure of friendship should not be proximity, but the fruits that the relationship bears.

When my grandmother was a young woman, she struck up what would become a lifelong friendship with her pen pal in England. They carried on for decades, getting to know each other intimately through the honesty of the written word. I truly believe that what we see as a result of social media today is the newest version of that. Just as she did, I get to reach around the world and find like-minded people. The only difference is that instead of writing letters and waiting on the postman, we can trade IMs in real time.

One of the benefits of an online friendship is how much easier it is to be boldly yourself from the very beginning. The same anonymity that allows internet trolls the license to stir up trouble also affords us the ability to speak freely. We reach out with only our thoughts and emotions and the words we choose to convey them. The people we meet can judge whether to befriend us based on what we say and how they see us treat other people we meet online. The bonds we develop are exactly as honest as we are.

When conversations aren't bound by time or space, they can run for days, picking up and slowing down according to convenience. Have to make dinner? Take the computer with you and type with your one clean pinky. Need to run a few errands? Go. The conversation will wait until you are back home and ready to jump back in. Lives don't have to pause for y'all to hang out the same way they do for real-life meet-ups. Online friendships are more fluid and forgiving. They're also easier to end. If either of you doesn't like what the other has to say, you can end the conversation and everyone walks away pretty much unscathed.

All friendships, online or in person, have to start with common ground. We must have a foundation upon which to build. Faith traditions, motherhood, owning the same breed of dog, a love of political debate, appreciation of a good pun — online or face-to-face, it starts the same way. We have to have something to get us talking, and then keep the conversation going.

Ten years ago, I was the stay-at-home mother of three small children, and I went online looking for another grown-up voice. The isolation of spending eight to ten hours of each day with only my children for company had me craving intelligent conversation. I needed to talk about serious subjects, and the people who wrote and read blogs were ready to indulge me.

Gradually, those bloggers I knew began to form into a loose and then a tight-knit community of mostly women Catholic writers. Years later, most of the original group has stopped blogging, but the community we built is still alive and thriving on Facebook, Twitter, Instagram, and Snapchat. We all follow one another, and the conversations we've been having for nearly a decade are still going on.

Any relationship is going to evolve and alter along with the changes of our season in life. Where once I was calling out into the great unknown in search of someone — anyone — to talk to, now I have a dozen or more acquaintances and friends needing only for me to step back to the keyboard. The once small children have grown into adults and teenagers, and the witty banter bounces back and forth in my house. Now the voices I once longed to hear are right under my roof. Now I'm looking for people to challenge me, to engage in a deeper discussion, to comfort and be comforted, and someone with whom to pray.

The people I now gather with online are those who are pursuing dreams beyond parenthood. We are seeing the time of raising small children coming to an end for us, and we are eagerly discussing what adventures will come next.

The rules

While the internet can be a great place to find your tribe, it's not all Pollyanna dancing through the daisies. There can be some crazy and unstable people out there, and it wouldn't be right to discuss online friendships without also talking about online safety. There are catfish online pretending to be someone they're not, creepy predators looking for prey, and lunatics looking to inflict their own brand of instability on an unsuspecting world. What can you do to keep the bad guys from finding you when so much time online is spent talking to strangers? (Sorry, Mom, I did listen when you told me not to. The world just looked very different back then.)

I wish that I could say everyone I've met online was as great as Leah and Éamonn, but, sadly, that's not the case. A couple of years ago, I met Jim in a Catholic theology group on Facebook. We shared the same point of view on the magisterium (gotta be faithful to it), the Protestant revolt, and a love of history. He sent me a friend request, and I accepted it. For more than a year he razzed me about rooting for the Oklahoma Sooners in football, opined about political posts, and seemed to be a good-natured guy. He was funny and harmless until he wasn't. After a few years of knowing each other online, he began sending me private messages that were not innocent or friendly. They crossed all kinds of lines with innuendos and personal comments, becoming more and more offensive when I didn't play along.

I called him on his nonsense, deleted conversations, and eventually unfriended and blocked him. That's when things got really ugly as he worked his way through our mutual acquaintances, saying the most despicable and disgusting things about me and my family. The man I had thought of with affection as a fellow Catholic struggling his way through life had become a nightmare who wanted to destroy me and any credibility I had.

Since Jim's attempt at slashing and burning his way through my friends list, I've changed some of the ways I interact with people online. I'm much more careful about the privacy settings I have in place on all of my accounts. When it comes to my personal accounts, I lock those babies down. If I don't know you in real life, you'd better be able to explain why I should add you to the pages I maintain for my closest friends and family. I started up public pages that I use for my writing and speaking work. While I may share bits and pieces of my life on those pages, I rarely post the whole story for public consumption.

I learned from my security-minded husband that Facebook, Instagram, and Snapchat all tag photographs with your location information. That means that if you take a picture at home, it's electronically tagged with your home address unless you change the settings to ghost mode. Not only do I not want the internet people to know where I live; I don't want them to know where my cute kids live, go to school, play, etc.

When I would get a friend/follow request from someone I didn't know or know well, I used to glance at their profile and pretty much accept anyone who had four or more friends in common with me. I'm bad with names, and chances were if we had enough people in common, I probably knew them too. Now I research like a crazy person. If there's a name and face I don't know, I start off with an IM that simply says: "I'm sorry. I can't remember how we know each other. Can you please remind me?" Anyone who doesn't answer is immediately gone. If their answer doesn't help me, I become a super-sleuth. I Google names and creep on profiles. If someone wants a front-row seat to my life, I want to know who they are.

The biggest change is in how I think of my online spaces. They are my digital living room, they are private, and I treat them that way. Just as I'm careful about who I let into my home, I think twice about who I let into my digital world, too. My real-life friends are always welcome, and that, of course, includes my real-life online friends. While there are a lot of great people out there with only good intentions, there are creepy catfishy types, too.

When you step out into online spaces and go searching for your people, keep your head about you, and keep yourself safe. A little common sense will help you weed through the riffraff. Hopefully someday soon you'll be watching a baptism from halfway around the world and waving like an idiot as your godchild is welcomed into the Church.

CHAPTER 14

My Useless Friends

*"I love people who make me laugh. I honestly think it's the
thing I like best, to laugh. It cures a multitude of ills.
It's probably the most important thing in a person."*
— Audrey Hepburn

M ost of the friendships that have filled my life have been
the result of proximity and convenience. Right time,
right place — boom, friendship. It was easier that way, and
with an ever-expanding brood of children, easy was what I had
time for.

There came a day when I realized that while I did not hate
the people I called my friends, I did not necessarily like them
all that much either, nor was I really sure that they honestly
liked me. We were in the habit of companionship rather than
truly being companions. In choosing friends for convenience,
I ended up with people who just happened to be there: Our
children played together. Their children took dance classes,
learned Latin, played sports, participated in Boy Scouts, etc.,
with my children. We were on committees together. We worked
together. We helped each other in our vocations.

They were great working friendships, but that was the
problem. They revolved around work. Eventually our lives
were so enmeshed that neither side could walk away because
to disentangle would be so disruptive. When you begin

choosing words carefully and tiptoeing around each other in order to maintain the status quo, that's not friendship. That's exhausting.

As much as moving to Texas a few years back was a disruption to our lives, it also gave me the invaluable opportunity to hit the reset button on my relationships. I decided to make the best of my chance to avoid relationships that are more work than pleasure, to consciously choose the people into whom I pour my time and energy, and to seek out the people whose company I genuinely enjoy. What I've learned is that if people have a use and a purpose, you're not really their friend, and they're probably not yours either.

At this point in my life, I'm only expending energy on keeping and seeking out friends who are anything except convenient. I've decided to place an emphasis on the quality of my friends rather than devoting myself to the people who require the least amount of time and effort. I have learned the importance of editing my inner circle, consciously drawing closer to those who bring joy to my life, and purposely disentangling myself from those who don't. As a result, it's taken a lot longer to build a tribe, but it's one that helps to sustain us all.

Being more selective in my relationships means that I have, and maintain, fewer friendships and have a lot more acquaintances these days. There are the people I meet on committees and the parents of my children's friends. I like them, and we are friendly. We chat and hang out, laugh and enjoy one another's company. We trade favors and recipes, but we are not truly close.

Then there are the few I love, a few from there and a few from here. The ones with whom I share my authentic self. The ones who bring nothing more than joy, peace, and comfort to my life. The ones without a purpose. They are the ones I keep for fun, the ones who make me truly happy just because I know them. They are my wonderful, beloved and truly "useless" friends. I hope they find me useless, too.

CHAPTER 15

Love the One You're With

"If you wanna find out who's a true friend, screw up or go through a challenging time ... then see who sticks around."
— Karen Salmansohn

D o you remember the stratification of high school society? In my small Texas town, the social outcasts were on the bottommost rung of the social ladder, and the cheerleaders and their football-player boyfriends were the very pinnacle of coolness. Most of us fell somewhere in between the kid who didn't bathe and the plastic perfection of the popular people. But whatever the case, we were all very aware of where we were on that totem pole. It was very easy to pick out the social climbers, the kids with their eyes on the prize of someday making it to the "cool kids'" table, especially at lunchtime. They always had "friends," but their relationships never seemed to last very long. They were predators on constant alert for an opening to move up the social scale. They weren't looking for friendships as much as opportunities.

It seems pretty mercenary in retrospect, but the reality is that we are all guilty of "trading up" at some point in our lives. While you may not aspire to Queen Bee status, the allure of the cool kids' table never completely goes away. We all have a natural desire to be liked and appreciated. As much as we don't want to pay attention to what anyone thinks, we're not designed to be lone wolves. We're made to find safety within our packs. We are created with a desire to belong, so we pay attention to whether our friends belong. There is a natural instinct which makes that seem important, even if it's just a momentary twinge.

As much as we may wish that adults would have outgrown this kind of stuff, too many people don't. Mean girls are everywhere, unfortunately, and most of us will experience them at least once in our lives. Even more unfortunately, too many of us have been the mean girls. We've rated our friends for coolness, cuteness, and what other people will think when they see us hanging out with our crew. What will they think of how we look? Will strangers laugh with us or at us? Will they want to join us? Will they want to be us?

You can only mentally shake yourself so many times for such nonsense before deciding enough already and working to change. While your brain may start running down those rabbit trails of its own volition, the best way to stop it in its tracks is to make an honest assessment of the people by your side. It might just be high time to show a little gratitude for the people who are already willing to put up with you.

One of my favorite sayings is "Other people's opinions of me are none of my business." Well, I'm here to tell you that other people's opinions of your friends aren't any of your business either. You're not in high school anymore, so stop looking for outside affirmation before you realize the value of what you have.

We all need a Sam

It would be awesome to have perfect friends — down-to-earth, not at all pretentious, but also really smart, and never, ever embarrassing — someone who just knows how to dress and to act in every social situation. You know that kind of person? People like that only exist in your imagination or in movies. They do the perfect things because it's all been planned out and scripted for them. The reason your favorite book and movie characters always know what to say is because it's taken extensive editing and tweaking to get it "just so." Real people don't have scriptwriters and editors for their everyday lives. We are flawed, so sometimes we're going to choose the wrong words or do the wrong things. We are all a little goobery once in a while, and for some of us it's a regular occurrence. If the never-goobery people exist, I haven't met them.

Even if you've already figured out that personal perfection is an impossible dream, most of us still have an idea of what our perfect friend would look like. It may be someone who reminds you of your bestie from elementary school. Remember how y'all spent a lot of years chasing Kevin around the playground trying to kiss him and then watching *The Last Unicorn* after school until you finally wore the VHS tape out? It sure would be great to have that kind of friend again, wouldn't it? Or maybe it's just the pipe dream of perfection that you've been carrying around in your head for your whole life. Either way, your chances are slim to none on finding the chupacabra of a BFF. It may exist out in the world somewhere, but if you're going to bet on long odds like that, you should be playing the lottery.

While you're waiting for your perfect BFF to come riding into town on a white horse, or at least driving a white Mustang, take a look at the friends you've already got. They may not be the knuckle-draggers you think they are. When I was eight years old and dreaming about my life as a grown-up, I pictured myself surrounded by glamorous friends. It was the 1980s, so the us in my mind had amazing fur coats, big hair, bigger diamonds, and layers of flawless eye shadow.

That is about as far from the fresh-faced, come-as-you-are group of friends I now have as you can possibly get. We are not as fancy as the women I thought we'd be, and we're definitely not as cool either. Every one of us is a bit odd and a little quirky — but by this point in our lives, most of us have made peace with that.

It's taken me a lot of life to accept that appearances don't count for much of anything, except in photographs. I've had to learn to love my friends for the people they are instead of trying to re-create them as the people I want them to be. I learned that looking for plastic perfection didn't make me happy, when what I really wanted was Sam. If you'll excuse me a *Lord of the Rings* (movie) nerd moment over here, Samwise Gamgee and Frodo Baggins are the greatest tale of friendship in modern literature. Of all the people that Frodo could have brought with him on his journey with the Ring, Sam was not the most impressive person who could have been taken along. Frodo knew everyone — elves, wizards, kings, and dwarves. (Let's take a moment to appreciate the beauty that is Legolas for a moment, shall we?) Frodo had the greatest and the bravest characters imaginable by his side as he began his journey, and he also had Sam.

Sam wasn't cool. In the movies, he was a bit on the chubby side and didn't seem all that bright. He was the gardener in the Baggins' garden. Unlike the other hobbits, he wasn't motivated by an epic journey. He wasn't interested in the heroism of accompanying the Ring to its eventual destruction. He didn't need to have songs written about him and his name remembered forever. He went along because Frodo was his friend, and he'd been asked. By the end of the tale, it was Sam, the "fat lump," mocked as inadequate even by Smeagol, who was the greatest hero of them all. Inside his humble being was a tower of strength and a deep well of bravery just waiting to be called upon.

Sam isn't the hero in spite of being ordinary. He's the hero precisely because he is ordinary. He's the vanilla ice cream of the whole story, in the background and overshadowed by everyone around him. He's also the one to walk through Mordor. We are surrounded in life by people who are ordinary like Sam. They may not be fat hobbits with hairy feet, but they are their own version of vanilla. A genuine hero could be hidden inside any one of them.

My grandmother has said that people are a lot like fish: they will jump at anything new and shiny. She's right, of course. We all like things that are new and exciting. It's what makes us turn our interest away from, or even drop, the friends we have in favor of the new person we met last night. It can be very tempting to fall into social climbing by association, or to succumb to the lure of the shiny and new, and ignore the ordinary beauty of the relationships you already have.

What if instead of searching for the people of your tribe out in the great wide somewhere, you looked a little closer to home at the people who are already in your social circle? It might just be that you've had a Sam hanging right beside you all along. In the immortal words of Ferris Bueller: "Life moves pretty fast. If you don't stop and look around once in a while, you could miss it." Have you stopped to look around lately? You might just be missing something — or, even worse, someone.

CHAPTER 16

Benefit of the Doubt

"You don't have to assume the worst about everyone, either.
The world isn't always out to get you."
— Sarah Dessen, *Lock & Key*

I t's a sad fact of life that if you spend enough time with someone, eventually they're going to do or say something that not only rubs you the wrong way but hurts your feelings or offends you. The fact that it happens is out of your hands. You can't control it. What happens next, on the other hand, is entirely up to you.

I nearly lost a friend once when she walked in on me and my friend Andrea telling what can only be described as racist jokes. She was mortally offended and decided on the spot that she could no longer be friends with anyone as reprehensible as we were. The incident was especially awkward since Andrea is black. Never once did it cross this friend's mind that there might be more to what was going on than what she knew.

Despite the popularity of the saying to the contrary, what you see isn't always what you get. Our friend was the victim of missing information. Sometimes our eyes and ears, and our perception of what they see and hear, is just flat-out wrong. I've learned from my own life that if someone I know, like, and respect suddenly does something completely out of character, it's possible that I was completely wrong about who they are.

But it's much more likely that I was just missing a key piece of information.

Had our friend given us the benefit of the doubt from the get-go, she'd have found out that Andrea and I were working on a paper for a minority studies class on racial stereotypes in comedy. We had been watching comedies from the past sixty years with stereotypes that skewered nearly every ethnic group. While those stereotypes would never be accepted in today's society, many of the jokes were screamingly funny, and we couldn't help but laugh as we discussed and wrote about the things we had seen.

While we don't intentionally run around trying to think the worst of people, many of us have been conditioned to assume bad intentions. We convict people long before the thought that there might be an innocent explanation ever crosses our minds. It may be our first instinct, but people — and especially our friends — deserve better than our condemnation in the absence of proof. Habitual flash judgment is a choice that we are making, one that we, as Christians, ought to resist. Instead of jumping to conclusions, we should be jumping to the benefit of the doubt.

To offer someone the benefit of the doubt means choosing to believe good instead of bad about her, when it could really go either way. It means to lean a little toward her side and assume that she is a basically decent person until proven otherwise. When you give your friends the benefit of the doubt, you give them the chance to explain themselves and to let their character speak for itself in spite of a bad first impression, a questionable circumstance, a slip of the tongue, or just flat out failure.

The circumstances in someone's life can influence and change their behavior in unpredictable ways. For instance, I have a friend, Kara, whom I have talked to or texted almost every day for the past thirteen years. She is as close to me as my own shadow, but there was a time when I disappeared from her without a word. In 2006, our daughter Bernadette was stillborn. I managed to hold myself together for her silent birth and the funeral that followed, and Kara was right there, offering me love and support. Then, one day, I woke up and began to mourn. The grief and emotional fatigue left me too drained to deal with anyone who didn't live in my house. Kara called multiple times a day, and I would look at the caller ID and set the ringing phone back down again. I had no energy to speak, and no desire to listen. It was all I could do just to exist.

After a few weeks, Kara began calling less and less. She was sure that she had somehow hurt my feelings and that I no longer wanted her in my life. She wracked her memory, searching for anything she could have done that would justify how profoundly silent I had become toward her. If I could have explained my absence from her life, she would have understood it, but at the time, I just couldn't.

Luckily for both of us, Kara is a wise and patient woman. While my disappearing act had hurt her, she was willing to wait until I came back to life and reached out to her once more. When I explained that intense grief and an abrupt hormone drop had run over me like a Mack truck, it all made sense to her. She accepted the circumstance behind my silence, and our friendship moved on unscathed.

Circumstances are everything when your friends become unpredictable or start behaving weirdly. If you can withhold judgment until you learn what those circumstances are, you can often hang on to the friendship. Admitting that you've been hurt or made uncomfortable and giving someone the benefit of the doubt is not mutually exclusive. It's not an either-or proposition; it can definitely be a both-and kind of thing.

Looking at a friend's history can also help to put things into perspective. Tigers don't change their stripes very often, and the best predictor of future behavior will always be past behavior. If a friend has a history of telling lies, you probably should be more skeptical of that person than you are of the friend who's generally a straight shooter. But keep in mind that people have been known to change. Saint Paul got knocked to his knees and went from being an arrogant jerk to becoming a pretty stand-up guy. So, if you have reason to hang your hat on hope, you may just get your wish.

One final thing — offering people the benefit of the doubt is different from living in a state of denial. Turning a blind eye or inventing reasons and stories to excuse bad behavior is not charitable. Nor is it beneficial to either one of you. And because friendship is supposed to be mutually beneficial, failing to address problems that arise undermines the purpose of being friends at all.

CHAPTER 17

Stay within the Lines – Creating Healthy Boundaries

"Boundaries aren't about trying to control someone or make them change. Boundaries are about establishing how you want to be treated, self-preservation in a chaotic or dangerous environment, and a path to healthy relationships."
— Sharon Martin, LCSW

Like all relationships, friendships function best when there are clear physical and emotional boundaries in place. For the most part, boundaries within a friendship occur organically — they grow and adapt as the relationship moves along. You figure out things such as when to call and when to text, when you each need a little space and when you want your friends around you, what topics to avoid, and what things drive each of you up the ever-loving wall.

There are some boundaries that are universally understood (or should be) in any relationship. These no-brainers include things such as:

Don't ask me to do anything immoral — I may like you, but I won't go to hell for you.
No emotional manipulation — Play with me, but don't play with my emotions.

Don't gossip — No telling tales out of school. If I've entrusted you with the truths of my life, they're not for public consumption. If you need to share someone's secrets, share your own.

Don't use me — Friends should not be a means to an end. I'm happy to be useful, but that doesn't mean that you can use me.

Be honest, but kind — Bambi's BFF Thumper said it best: "If you can't say something nice, don't say nuthin' at all." If you can't put it nicely, you might want to sit on it until you can figure out how. And don't lie.

No verbal abuse — Sticks and stones may break your bones, but words can break your heart.

No physical abuse — Friendship shouldn't hurt, and it definitely shouldn't leave bruises. Someone who hurts you should be called a criminal and not a companion.

No cheaters allowed — Don't flirt (or sleep with) my man. Period. Just no.

Don't mess with my kids — I will hunt you down, and you don't want to see what happens next.

After the no-brainers, also known as how not to end up on a hit list, it's up to you to decide what you're personally comfortable with. These aren't things with a moral weight to them; they're about your own personal preferences and comfort level — things such as:

Do you like to talk on the phone? If so, how often? I have a friend whom I speak with daily, and often more than once in a day, while there are others I speak to on the phone only once in a blue moon. On the whole, though, I like talking on the phone. I enjoy hearing the voices of the friends I miss the most. It makes them seem not so far away.

Do you prefer texting? Some people are too busy for phone conversations, or would rather save their talking for the times when they are face to face with their friends. Others are introverts who get "touched out" pretty quickly and thrive on the space that texting gives them. Whatever the reason, they would rather text any day of the week, and are shocked when the phone rings with a call instead of buzzing with a message.

Do you like drop-in guests, or do you want people to call ahead? The extrovert in me loves to have people pop in any time and for any reason. It makes me unreasonably happy. My BFF is even allowed to just walk right in without knocking first. My husband, on the other hand, is uncomfortable with the disruption a pop-by can cause in his schedule. This means that my friends know they are welcome any time he's at work or out of town, but if he's home, they need to give us a heads-up first.

Subtle hints or just say it straight out?

Most of the personal-preference boundaries that we set are put in place through subtle behaviors that we may not even be conscious of. For example, if your friend is a phone chatterer and you prefer texting, when he calls you, let it roll to voice mail and then text back "What's up?" Unless he's a box of rocks, he's going to quickly catch on to the idea that you are easier to get hold of via text message. If you have a friend who LOVES discussing politics and digging deep into the most pressing topics of the day, but the idea of dissecting each other's stance on the latest controversy leaves you feeling slightly nauseated, you can change the subject whenever the topic arises, and he'll get the message that that's a no-go area for you.

Or you can be a freaking grown-up.

Instead of playing the passive-aggressive I'm-going-to-text-you-instead-of-answering game, you could just say, "I get it that you like to talk on the phone, but I just don't have the time to chitchat/phone calls wake up the baby/often I can't stop what I'm doing to pick up/I'm an introvert and I just hate the phone." Just put the truth on the table and see what happens. Any friend worth having is going to appreciate being told the truth instead of being expected to pick up on your subtle (or not-so-subtle) clues. Games belong on the playground or on the gaming system; they don't belong in your friendships.

Laying it out there plainly is especially important when your boundary is a no-go area for you. If you refuse to be around someone when they are smoking, or if you are uncomfortable with course or crude language, for instance, you owe it to your friends to be upfront about that.

When boundaries get crossed

Nobody is a perfect friend, and lines are going to get stepped over every now and again. Whether one of the no-brainer, universal kind of boundaries or just a personal no-go rule that you have been clear about in the past, you will have to discern whether you want to discuss this with your friend and give her the chance to make amends. If it's something that happens repeatedly, you may decide to end things.

If it's a personal-preference boundary that's been crossed, you will have to decide whether it's worth addressing, or whether there is a compromise that would make both of you happy. Personal preferences are going to evolve and change within the relationship over time. Your "rules" will apply until they don't. There may come a day when the friend whose phone calls you used to let roll over to voice mail becomes the person you talk to on a daily basis, or even multiple times a day. The boundary you need to have with yourself is "Don't be so inflexible that it costs you your friends."

Boundaries are part of any healthy relationship. They help to keep both of you feeling safe, comfortable, and valued. Boundaries should not cause power struggles or become a means of exercising control. They should not be a source of friction or foster tension within your relationship. When the boundaries in your relationship are healthy and fair, they give both of you the freedom to relax and be yourselves, which is the whole point of being friends in the first place.

CHAPTER 18

Friends for a Reason or a Season

"People don't come into our lives by chance.
If they're there, they're crossing your path for a reason."
— Linda Lane

M ost of us don't go out and specifically search for temporary friends. If we are making the effort to consciously look for our people, we hope to find someone who's going to be around long enough to participate in life with us. Forming new relationships requires a tremendous amount of energy and effort. Even when it's fun work, it's still work. If we knew upfront that the bonds we were forming came with an expiration date, I wonder how many of us would think it was worth the effort. A well-known quote suggests friendship can be divided into three categories: those there for a reason, those for a season, and those who are around for a lifetime.

The lifetime friends are, of course, the ones who will end up having the greatest influence on the people we are and ultimately become. I'm lucky that one of my lifetime friends is my younger brother, Doug. While we've been siblings from his beginnings, we became friends when he was in his twenties. He is one of the best friends I've ever had. We challenge and encourage each other, not just in our daily and professional lives, but also in how we live our faith.

Not every friendship is going to be as close as a brother-turned-best-friend. In fact, it would be exhausting to have that level of intimacy and involvement in the lives of all the people we call friends. There are some friends who are in our lives for definite reasons. Sometimes, God places people in our lives, or we deliberately choose to have them in our inner circle, because of the lessons we can learn and teach each other, or because we come to rely on each other's expertise.

My daughter's ability to walk became impeded, and she began using a wheelchair a few years ago. In our quest for answers, I reached out to all the medical people in my social media circles. One of the women I knew through blogging turned out to be a medical diagnostician. We got to know each other over the following year, often IMing in the wee hours of the night when I was up with the baby and she was at work. She taught me about medical proof and what questions to ask, and we learned about each other's lives. It was a work friendship that we both enjoyed — me looking for answers and her getting to help solve a great mystery. When we finally found a diagnosis through a strange happenstance, the reason behind our friendship was gone. Our late-night conversations tapered off gradually into silence. The friendship recently started up again now that she's a first-time mom with all kinds of questions and worries, and this time I'm lending my expertise to her.

Sometimes relationships are built on what you know, and other times their foundation rests on being in the same season of life. The "bonds of sisterhood" between members of a sorority, the camaraderie mothers of preschoolers share at the local MOPS group, even the hyper-competitive tenuous bond of "dance moms" all have their foundational elements in being in the same stage of life in the same places at the same time. There is a comfort and an ease that is found in friendships that begin in being in the same stage of life together.

My ninety-six-year-old grandmother tells stories of being a young housewife in Texas in the 1950s. Motherhood way back in the day was much more of a team sport. The cookie-cutter bungalows which lined the neighborhood streets were filled with young families of GIs recently returned from fighting World War II. It was the middle of the baby boom, and all the women living up and down the streets were young wives with chubby-cheeked children. They all did laundry on Tuesdays and Saturdays, helping one another with hanging sheets and unmentionables on the lines, while their babies slept in the shade of a grizzled oak tree. My grandma still tells about these women, in and out of one another's houses, a giggling, hard-working feminine cooperative of hospitality. "It was a season," she always says with a wistful smile. "It was just a short season in a long life."

Eventually, most of those 1950s housewives moved off that street. Life and careers carried them away, and the magic of those early days of motherhood, when the world was newly at peace, faded into the hard work of farm and family. Grandma only kept in touch with one of her war-bride friends throughout the years, but that doesn't make the friendships she had any less meaningful.

There are times in our lives when we look at the people around us and cannot imagine that there will ever be a time when they won't be near and dear to us. We joke about taking up a whole wing together at the old folks' home and how we're going to terrorize the nurses in delight. It's difficult to imagine a moment when our people will no longer be our people, but instead will have become just people we used to know. Luckily, most of us aren't gifted with prophetic vision, and even though we might suspect which friends will last and which ones will be lost along the way, we don't really know for sure. And that's a good thing. Not knowing how things will be in the end allows us to give unreservedly of ourselves now and to enjoy our current friends.

The fact that most friendships end at some point says next to nothing about their value. Some of our very best don't last for a lifetime — it's a part of friendship's normal life cycle, and ours. The kind of friendships we have, whether for a reason, a season, or life, does not define us as people. Having friendships that fade or end abruptly doesn't doom all of our friendships to following the same pattern or narrative. It simply means that your life has moved on, and there's now space in your life for a new chapter and new people.

CHAPTER 19

Saying Goodbye

"Growing apart doesn't change the fact that for a long time we grew side by side; our roots will always be tangled."
— Ally Condie

As much as we wish it weren't so, sometimes friendships die. Some will wither on the vine before they ever reach their full potential. Others fall victim to changes in life or lifestyle, moves, job changes, new babies, or kids going off to college. Even close friendships can grow stale, or tempers may flare up in an explosion that destroys too much to rebuild. Or, a friendship may end for no discernible reason at all. Whatever the case, losing a friend stinks and is often accompanied by a pain that lingers, even for years.

While we often toss the word "friend" around, losing a friend is more than just the absence of someone you used to know. Depending on the depth of the relationship, it can be as serious a loss in your life as a divorce or a death. That's because our friendships give us a feeling of being valued, important, and understood. They root us within a community and provide us with a safety net. The closest of friends can be closer to us than our relatives. For many of us, they become a family that we have chosen for ourselves. So why isn't the loss of friendship treated like the big deal that it is? And why are so many of us flat-footed when it comes to finding closure?

If you lose a friendship as the result of what's going on in your friend's life, there's not much to do except to accept that sometimes life happens. Tell your friend goodbye, in person if you can, and wish them well. If there is no one at fault, you might want to think about leaving the door open in case they find their way back to you. You honor your good friendship when you pray for the other person's well-being and happiness as they move on.

A good deal of soul-searching goes on when we lose a friend, and that's a good thing. Some of the questions we ought to ask ourselves include: Did I take my friend for granted? Was I rude, condescending, or dismissive? Was I an emotional vampire sucking up all their emotional energy?

If you realize that you've in any way contributed to the demise of the relationship, you owe your friend an apology. Remember that even if they're absolutely, totally, and completely in the wrong, you might not be 100 percent blameless. So, say you're sorry, and mean it. It may not be enough to salvage the relationship, but it could be enough to deflate some of the anger or hurt. If at all possible, you shouldn't leave that kind of negativity behind you. Try to make amends if you can. You owe it to both of you.

Sometimes, though, it is your own fault. As much as we would like that not to be true, sometimes there's no one to blame but ourselves, and we know it. What can you do when you know that the blame lies squarely upon your own shoulders? Even worse, how should you react when you know that your friend is absolutely right to walk away? If you've done something especially scandalous, there's not much to do except admit guilt, ask for forgiveness, and pray for your friend's happiness as you watch her walk away. Don't grovel or beg. If it's going to end, then let it be clean. Give the gift of making it easy to part ways.

Losing your friend is the price you may have to pay for bad behavior, but what you do once you've paid the I-was-a-jerk tax will decide whether it's going to happen again. Have you learned your lesson? First off, you've got to figure out what happened and why, and be willing to admit it. It's painful to acknowledge that our behavior could possibly have damaged someone we care about, but you can't change until you are honest with yourself. Confession is good for the soul, so accept responsibility for your behavior to your former friend, and then go fess up to a priest.

I once lost a very dear friend because what was happening in my own life — and it was a lot going on — blinded me to what was going on in hers. I used her for emotional support and offered none in return. She was right to walk away from me, and as much as I hated to see her go, I knew she was right to leave. I miss her terribly, but am forever thankful for the lesson that the demise of our friendship taught me — that friendships are reciprocal. If I need a therapist, I should hire a therapist.

Whatever the reason for the split, let the break be a clean one. Resist the urge to spy on Facebook walls or creep on Instagram. Let your former friend go completely. Don't cling to the memory of the relationship that used to be. We each have a finite number of people we can care about at any given time in our lives. If you're hanging on to a former friend, it's not only disrespectful to someone who can't or no longer wishes to be a part of your life; it's also filling up a valuable slot that could be filled by someone new.

Is it time for you to end it?

There are some friends who will be in your life until one of you dies, and others who will last only a short season or two. Some will help you to become a better person, and others will show you by their example the kind of person you don't want to be. No relationship is going to be smooth sailing all the time, but how do you tell the difference between when you should soldier on and mend those ties and when it's time to cut them loose? There are reasons it might be time to say goodbye.

You've changed

Two roads diverged in the woods, and you took different paths. People change. That's neither a good nor a bad thing; it's just a thing that happens. God places people in your life so you can learn from others. When you and a particular friend have grown beyond each other, you've reached the relationship's expiration date. If you're both ducking phone calls and hiding behind the grocery-store displays to avoid the other, it's already over. Let it drift away. It could be that letting go will be the best thing you can do for each other.

The clinging vine

It's one thing for friends to enjoy each other's company and want to be together; it's something else entirely when your friend never gives you the chance to be alone. If your right-hand girl becomes your constant shadow and starts to rely on you too much, you may have crossed the line between friendship and codependence.

In a healthy relationship, your lives will have parts that intersect, and others that are separate from each other. With a clinging-vine type of person, that time alone never seems to happen. Even your getaways are punctuated by questions of where you are and what you're doing. Before you know it, you're quietly covering up any plans that don't include her or figuring out the best way to word things so that you don't hurt your friend's feelings.

If you want to continue the friendship, you can try discussing her clinginess and ask for some space without embarrassing your friend or shaming her. If, after talking it over, the smothering continues, walking away from the friendship may be the only way for you to get the separation that you need.

It can be hard to end a relationship with a clinging vine. For starters, she won't want to let you go. It can also be difficult for you to break the habit of hanging out with her. The hero worship of a vine type can be extremely flattering, and being the center of someone else's attention can become an addiction, too. It's not good for either one of you. If you leave a clinging vine behind, do it kindly but completely. Don't leave any hope that you'll be coming back.

Drama queen

Most of us don't realize we've become friends with a drama queen until it's too late. We've already been sucked into the excitement of her world, and it's going to be a thrilling ride through the adventures of her life. Drama queens tend to be fun, charismatic, and exciting people to be around.

The drama queen, however, is an emotional chameleon. Her shifting moods and firecracker temper mean that you're never going to be bored with her around, but it also makes it extremely difficult to have peace. There will come a day when your emotional attention span for her drama is going to burn itself out. If she's not going to get help to change things, there are three options left to you: (1) embrace the drama and live in the moment; (2) set clear boundaries and limit your contact; or (3) be like Elsa and just let it go.

If you've decided that the only way to keep your sanity is to lose the relationship, be ready for the backlash. You've seen your friend at work, so you know that ending things is going to cause, you guessed it, DRAMA. She's your friend, so you owe her an explanation. Just don't be surprised if she can't hear what you've said. Remember that the tragedies of her life are almost never her own fault, so this newest chapter is going to be all on you. If she gets spinning hard enough, she may take all of your mutual friends with her. Know upfront that that may happen, and console yourself that her histrionics are the price of admission to a calmer and saner life.

The vampire

Vampires are a spinoff of the drama queen and are a big enough deal to get a heading all to themselves. Vampires are friends who consistently take more than they give. They are more of a drain than a support. There are two distinct types: the emotional vampire and the resource sucker.

We all have known resource suckers in our lives, and chances are you have a few in your family as well. The sucker always seems to have an emergency and need something — a babysitter, a ride, to borrow your grandmother's necklace, to borrow money. They are always on the taking side and rarely if ever available to help. They may offer to help, but somehow it just doesn't seem to work out.

The emotional vampire will leave your stuff alone. It's you they feed on — your energy, your attention, your support. What may have started as an emotionally healthy relationship somehow became completely one-sided. All the conversations seem to focus on the minutiae of the vampire's life. You may find yourself wondering, "When do we get to talk about me?" It's going to be a rare thing, if it ever happens at all. The vampire isn't really interested in your life, except in terms of how it relates to them.

Sometimes vampirism is a habit your friend may have fallen into unintentionally. She gets used to being the center of attention and forgets to share the spotlight. If that's the case, an honest heart-to-heart conversation is in order. She may just need to be made aware of the problem in order to fix it.

But if your friendship is constantly taking you away from your family and other friends, and stealing the peace of your household, it may be time to walk away. It's never okay for your friend's life to consume yours. Her kids shouldn't see you more often than your own kids do. If your time and resources are being sucked dry, or if contact with your friend leaves you feeling depressed, overwhelmed, or filled with anxiety, it's time to take a break or let the friendship go. You can't have a healthy life if you're running on empty.

The abuser

You might have a friend you hang out with and find that the more time you spend in her company, the worse you feel about yourself. Backhanded compliments, sarcastic snipes, or plain old insults (even if she's "just kidding" and says them with a smile) are verbal abuse. Anyone who leaves you feeling insecure and self-conscious is not your friend, and not the type of person you want in your life.

I had a friend in high school who liked to throw things when she got mad. The rage would overtake her, and she would become a screaming, throwing blur, and you'd better hope that you could duck. It wasn't until I was an adult that I realized her tantrums were actually a form of emotional and physical abuse to anyone nearby. She willingly put all of us in physical danger because she was angry. It was frightening to me back then, and I've often wondered if she got help to deal with her anger. I'll never know because I'm not her friend any longer. There is no excuse for this kind of behavior, and you shouldn't accept it. If your friendship is ever physically abusive, end it immediately. If you don't feel safe doing so, please call the authorities. Local police will be more than happy to end the friendship for you.

Nobody has the right to hurt you emotionally, verbally, or physically. You not only have a right to safety; you have a moral obligation to protect yourself. The abuser is not your friend. Ever.

Ending a friendship is never easy. It's the last step any of us ever wants to take. But sometimes, it's best for everyone involved. If at all possible, give your soon-to-be-ex-friend the gift of closure — knowing exactly what happened and why you've chosen to end things. Honor the memory of the friendship by keeping private anything that was entrusted to you, and don't speak badly of your former friend to anyone else. The ending of a friendship doesn't mean that the history you have shared wasn't important, or that you never cared about each other. It just means that it's time for both of you to move on.

CHAPTER 20

Friendship with God

*"Acquire the habit of speaking to God as if you were alone
with him, familiarly and with confidence and love, as to the
dearest and most loving of friends."*
— Saint Alphonsus Liguori

When I was a young Catholic girl in a small Texas town, it never occurred to me to think of Jesus as my friend. My Protestant friends would talk about having a "personal relationship" with Jesus in the same way they talked about being born again, so it wasn't something the Catholic me ever thought of as necessary. I had made friends with the saints, and felt a glowing love for the Blessed Mother, but the bleeding form of Jesus on the cross was too intimidating for me to look at and think "friend." We would talk in CCD class (Sunday school for you young pups) about how "God so loved the world that he gave his only begotten Son," and while I was one of "the world," it didn't feel like a personal thing.

If Jesus was too awe-inspiring to be my friend, the idea of having any personal relationship with the Creator of the universe was laughable. What on earth could the God of Everything possibly want to do with insignificant me? I was a small-town girl who liked the boys too much, broke any rule I came near, and wasn't sure that I believed there was a God at all. And even if there was, why would the One who could have

his pick of anyone on earth for a friend choose me? Seriously,
Mother Teresa or me? That's not even a question that needed to
be asked. The answer was obvious.

It wasn't until I held my second baby (and then third and
fourth and all the babies after that) that I understood the
weirdness of a parent's love. It isn't a choice between loving the
easy one and loving the difficult one — there's just love, and
it spreads itself around. I had wandered away and then come
back to the Catholic Church with a healthy fear of God, but
my love of him was only frightened. I talked to the saints and
asked them to go talk to God for me. I was still unworthy, in
my own mind, to approach the throne of the most-high God.

It took a VeggieTales episode on Saint Patrick to change
my approach to God. The Saint Patrick character quips that
he prays "a hundred times a day. It's a lot, but it's cool." I sat in
deep thought for a while after that. A hundred times a day. It's
a lot, but it's cool.

How on earth could anyone pray a hundred times a day?
I consulted the ultimate authority on everything, Google, and
found that Pat really did pray that much. But how could he
have time for that? What with crossing myself, the formality,
and the whatnots, prayer as I understood it takes a really long
time. Then it occurred to me: maybe Patrick wasn't using the
whatnots. Maybe a hundred times a day was less about awe-
struck worship and more about a long-running conversation. I
wasn't even sure that such a thing was kosher. But I didn't have
anything to lose, so I tried it.

That first day, I chattered about everything. I talked to God
as I scrambled eggs for breakfast and as I chased the naked
baby through the house with a diaper. I talked about the dog
who refused to be housebroken and the ache for a friend who
had moved away. I talked and hoped he listened, and I went to
bed that first night feeling heard. So I did it again the next day.
It took a week for me to run out of things to say, and then I just
hung out in the silence with him … and listened.

As this tiny spark of a relationship grew, I began reading
anything and everything I could about God. He wasn't the

loudest talker I'd ever known, so I found answers elsewhere. I cracked open the dusty Bible on my shelf and found the description for the friendship I wanted with God. Right there in the beginning, in Genesis, God was walking and talking with Adam and Eve in the Garden. Walking and talking isn't trembling in fear; it's companionship. This wasn't a formal or distant thing, but an intimate and loving relationship between Creator and creation. A friendship without a scrap of guilt or fear (or clothing) between them. It's what he wanted from all of his creation from the very beginning.

"He walks with me, and he talks with me, and he tells me I am his own" goes the hymn. Walking and talking like Adam and Eve in the Garden, like Patrick in his days of slavery and evangelization, like Saint Thérèse and her little way. Friendship with God means worship and awe, yes, but also love and companionship.

So where does such a friendship even begin?

You just start talking. You say "hi" and let the conversation begin. You go and sit in a pew in a church, ideally before the Blessed Sacrament, and spend some time doing what a friend of mine calls "Son bathing." Drink in the peace of being in his presence.

Through his Son, God has reached out to us and offered us a relationship that is more than awe and worship. "No longer do I call you servants," Jesus said, flat-out, "but I have called you friends" (Jn 15:15). Jesus was the friend of sinners, who ate with thieves and whores (let's just call the tax collectors and prostitutes what they really were) and had such love and compassion for them.

For a long time, I got hung up on his pronouncement that those people who are his friends keep his commands. It sounded like strings attached, as if he were saying, "I'll love you as long as you do what I want you to do." Maybe it's that I'm many years beyond the rebellion of high school and college, but now I see that in a different light. I, too, have a Code of Conduct for what would be unacceptable to me in my friends — things such as abuse, infidelity, and dishonesty. I say to my friends, "I want to be your person, and these are the boundaries for the kind of person I expect you to be."

Jesus has done the same thing. He has laid out the morals and ethics he expects of us and says: "If you're my friend, you'll try to live within this range of acceptable behavior. I won't abandon you if you don't, but you'd better be working on it." It's not about control, but about respect — respecting his personhood and his godhood.

But friendship doesn't start with rules; it starts with an introduction. It begins with hospitality, and welcoming each other into your homes, breaking bread together, and getting to know each other. It begins with prayer, Mass, confession, and Communion. It starts with looking for him in all the places where he can be found, and then allowing him the chance to just be a part of your life.

We all were created with two instinctive needs for companionship, one for our "tribe" of people, and the other for an intimate relationship with our Creator. When we don't have the people we need around us, we feel the ache of a hole in our lives, but when we don't have a relationship with God, it creates a more personal kind of longing deep within us.

The people we choose to bring into our lives bring with them fun, comfort, challenge, a safety net, companionship, and a myriad of other benefits. Our relationships with family and friends are so necessary to our lives that they have a measurable and demonstrable effect on our physical and mental health. In short, we are designed to belong within a tribe, a close-knit group of friends and family, that cares for us, our well-being, and our success in life. If we aren't fortunate enough to have a tribe already in place, then we have to go out and find one.

As amazing as the people we love are, they can never hope to fill the God-shaped hole that is inside us all. We each have a space in our soul that can only be filled with the love and presence of the most-high God. Until we invite him into relationship and companionship with us, that hole will remain, and we will always have an instinctive loneliness that no amount of socializing will be able to fix.

We need relationships with both people and God. Those relationships aren't just going to happen for you; you're going to have to do the work necessary to find them, and put in the effort to keep them healthy, close, and strong. It may seem like a daunting task, but, in reality, it's one you instinctively know how to do.

A Little Something from Grandma

My grandma always said that it wasn't really a visit with friends if you hadn't eaten anything, and that there was nothing better than something you had made with your own two hands. I know that not everyone is a cook these days, but Grandma's Deep-Dish Pie (it's really more of a cobbler) doesn't require very much skill at all. If the way to the heart is through the stomach, then here's a little shortcut for you with love from me and Grandma.

Deep-Dish Pie
Ingredients
2 cans pie filling, any flavor
3/4 stick butter
1 cup sugar
1 cup flour

1 cup milk
2 tsp baking powder
1 tsp vanilla

Directions: Grease casserole dish. Mix all ingredients but butter and filling together. Put in pan. Spoon pie filling on top and slice butter over the filling. Bake at 350 degrees for about an hour.

Yes, it is that easy. It looks weird, but the crust rises up through and around the fruit to make a lovely golden-brown cakelike top. Serve it with ice cream or a large mug of coffee. It's not the healthiest recipe out there, but so what? You're not looking for health food; you're hanging out with your friend.